★★★★ THE BEST ★★★★ FREE ATTRACTIONS
IN THE EASTERN STATES

by John Whitman

Meadowbrook Press
18318 Minnetonka Blvd. • Deephaven, MN 55391

*My thanks to all those people whose help and cooperation were essential in realizing **The Best Free Attractions:** Bert Berlowe, Greg Breining, Mary Cichy, Marcia Conley, Denise Hesselroth, Monty Mickelson, Mary Rockcastle, Amy Rood, Sue Veazie—and the thousands of people across the US who contributed their time and information so willingly.* J.W.

Printed in the United States of America
ISBN 0-915658-35-6
Copyright © 1981 by John Whitman

Editor: Kathe Grooms
Designer: Terry Dugan
Illustrator: John Shank
Production Manager: John Ware

CONTENTS

Free! That's the key. *The Best Free Attractions* is unlike any other travel guide you can find, because it lists hundreds of terrific travel attractions that don't cost a penny. You'll be amazed at what great things there are to do and see that are *still* free in this country.

You will find free zoos, aquaria and planetaria; hiking and biking trails; outdoor attractions like scenic wonders, parks, beaches and even free campsites; curiosities like ghost towns, reversible waterfalls, giant statues, UFO-sighting spots and folk art creations; wonderful festivals, fairs, plays, concerts and films; historic sites and museums; gardens, architectural sights and picnic spots; pro sports team practices, behind-the-scene tours and TV show tapings; plus parades, fireworks ... and more. There's something for everyone here!

Every entry in this book has been carefully evaluated and verified. Attractions that only let certain people in free (for example, kids or seniors) aren't listed—only those that are truly free for everybody. I've even found out when the free-entry days or periods fall for fee-charging attractions, and they're listed here as well.

The book is organized alphabetically by state and by towns within them. Each description is headed by the name of the nearest town. Attractions that are regional (like beaches) or scattered throughout the state (like free campsites) are listed in a separate category headed "Statewide." These listings follow the alphabetical town listings. When times are specified, they are for when the attraction is free (if no day is specified you can assume the hours apply seven days a week). The contact phone numbers and addresses are all accurate as we go to press, but be aware that they are changeable and call ahead if you're planning a special trip based on a single attraction. Also call ahead if you're planning a holiday excursion—holiday hours often differ from regular ones.

In these days of rising costs, you may find an attraction listed here as free which has begun to charge admission since we went to press. If you do find significant changes, please do let me know so I can change future listings and keep this book accurate. There's a page in the back of this book for your comments.

Take advantage of the free fun listed in this book. You'll experience an authentic slice of American life, unmarred by commercial hype. I hope you'll use *The Best Free Attractions* frequently ... and remember that good times *don't* have to be expensive!

CONNECTICUT

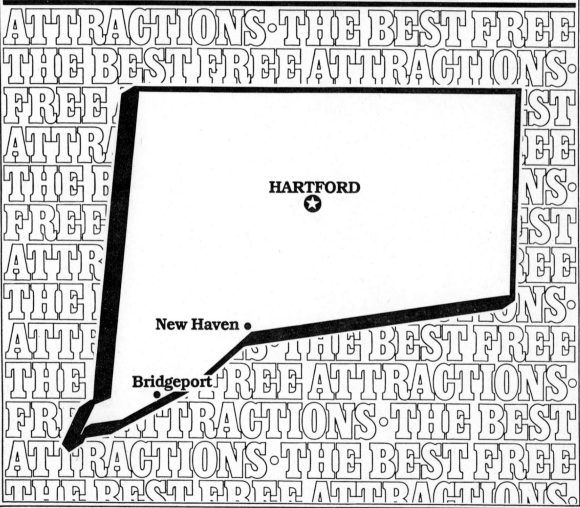

ATTRACTIONS·THE BEST FREE
THE BEST FREE ATTRACTIONS·
FREE
ATTR
THE B
FREE
ATTR
THE
ATTR
THE
FREE

HARTFORD

New Haven

Bridgeport

ATTRACTIONS·THE BEST FREE
THE BEST FREE ATTRACTIONS·

CONNECTICUT

Bridgeport

50,000-Piece Circus Model

Visit the original Circus City and you'll find the Barnum Museum. It has an extensive collection of clown props and costumes, an unwrapped mummy, an elaborate animated Swiss Village with 20,000 moving parts, and a hand-carved, animated five-ring miniature circus. The latter is 40 by 60 feet and is made up of 50,000 hand-carved pieces.

Time: Tues.-Sat., noon-5 p.m.; Sun., 2-5 p.m.
Place: 820 Main St.
Contact: (203) 576-7320

Colonial Furniture

The Museum of Art, Science and Industry is definitely worth visiting. It features an extremely fine collection of colonial furniture as well as circus memorabilia and exhibits on Connecticut Indians.

Time: Free Fri. only, 10 a.m.-5 p.m.
Place: 4450 Park Ave.
Contact: (203) 372-3521

Clinton

1789 Mansion

The Stanton House has 13 rooms furnished in late 17th- and early 18th-century pieces. The white, two-story home is an outstanding example of early American construction.

Time: June-Sept., Tues.-Sun., 2-5 p.m.
Place: 63 E. Main St.
Contact: (203) 669-2132

Essex

Authentic Inn

The Griswold Inn, the most attractive in the state, dates from 1776 and lies near the Connecticut River. British troops ate here before burning the American fleet in 1812. In the taproom and the main dining room is a notable collection of Currier and Ives prints.

Time: Best mid-afternoon, 2-5 p.m., to see the art.
Place: Main St.
Contact: (203) 767-0991 or 767-1812

Fairfield

Oldest Songbird Refuge

A haven for our feathered friends, the Birdcraft Museum has more than 4,000 specimen of wildlife and native birds. Its sanctuary, set aside in 1914, is said to be the oldest in the US.

Time: Sat., 10 a.m.-5 p.m.; Sun., noon-5 p.m.
Place: 314 Unquowa Rd.
Contact: (203) 259-0416

Greenwich

Handcarved Pipes

Indians gave Christopher Columbus his first cigar in 1492. You can sample free snuff as you tour tobacco displays in the US Tobacco Museum, with everything from French lithographs to hundreds of hand-carved pipes. A nice portrait of the aesthetic and addictive nature of the leaf.

Time: Tues.-Sun., noon-5 p.m.
Place: 100 W. Putnam Ave.
Contact: (203) 869-5531

Groton

Submarine Museum

If you're an underwater enthusiast, you'll want to stop in at the Submarine Museum and Library. It has an excellent collection of 75 sub models, periscopes and related gear.

Time: By appt.
Place: US Naval Submarine Base
Contact: (203) 449-3174

Guilford

Acres of Roses

In one of the world's largest and most lush greenhouses you can visit acres of roses, the main crop of William Pinchbeck, Inc. No regular tours are offered, but you can call ahead and arrange one.

Time: By appt., Mon.-Thurs., 8 a.m.-noon, 1-4 p.m.; Fri.-Sat., 8 a.m.-noon.
Place: 929 Boston Post Rd.
Contact: (203) 453-2186
Note: Please avoid the week before major holidays as a courtesy to the growers.

Hartford

Free Music

Hartford courts its musicians and music lovers. The city sponsors street festivals, noontime shows, the New England Fiddle Contest and Monday evening jazz concerts throughout the summer.

Time: Fiddle: Sat. of Mem. Day weekend, 10 p.m.-midnight. Jazz: late June-Aug., Mon., dusk. Call for schedules of other events.
Place: Bushnell Park.
Contact: (203) 727-1000 or 566-6016

Gothic Taj Mahal

It's said that Gore Vidal once labeled this State Capitol as a Gothic Taj Mahal. See whether you agree on a tour of this gold-domed edifice.

Time: Capitol: Mon.-Fri., 8:30 a.m.-5 p.m. Tours: June 15-Labor Day, 9:30 a.m.-3 p.m. every half hour; rest of year, call for appts.
Place: Capitol Ave.
Contact: (203) 566-3662

Wild Bill Hickok's Gun

The guns that won the West were made in the East—many in Hartford. Don't miss the rare collection of Colt pistols and firearms in the Connecticut State Library, which also features the table on which Lincoln signed the Emancipation Proclamation.

Time: Mon.-Fri., 8:30 a.m.-5 p.m.; Sat., 9 a.m.-1 p.m.
Place: 231 Capitol Ave.
Contact: (203) 566-3808

10,000 Roses

Don't miss Elizabeth Park if you're in the city in late June and early July. Over 500 varieties of roses totaling more than 10,000 plants are in full magnificent bloom at that time.

Time: Best: June 25-July 4, sunrise to sunset.
Place: Elizabeth Park, 915 Prospect Ave.
Contact: (203) 566-6320

View

The Travelers Tower soars 527 feet above the city. You'll have to climb 70 steps before you can catch the view from the observation room, but it's worth the effort.

Time: Apr.-Oct., Mon.-Fri., 8:30 a.m.-3:30 p.m., by appt. only.
Place: 1 Tower Sq.
Contact: (203) 277-2431

Rare Antiques

At the Connecticut Historical Society you'll find a collection of approximately 55 rare antiques, a dozen pieces dating back to the 17th and early

CONNECTICUT

Hartford

18th centuries. Silverware and Indian pottery round out the valuable displays.
Time: Mem. Day-Labor Day, Mon.-Fri., 1-5 p.m.; rest of year, Mon.-Sat., 1-5 p.m.
Place: 1 Elizabeth St.
Contact: (203) 236-5621

Audubon Masterpiece

The original volume of *Birds of America*, Audubon's masterpiece, can be viewed at the Trinity Watkinson Library. Because the folio is so valuable, it is not open to be examined on a casual basis. However, there's always one plate on display to the general public.
Time: By special arrangement.
Place: Trinity College campus.
Contact: (203) 527-3151, ext. 307

Litchfield

Ralph Earl's Works

The Litchfield Historical Society runs a small museum with quality exhibits. It has a notable collection of works by Ralph Earl.
Time: Mid-Apr.-mid-Nov., Tues.-Sat., 11 a.m.-5 p.m.
Place: South and East Sts.
Contact: (203) 567-5862

Family Hike

After taking the kids into the White Memorial Conservation Center to see the live owls, snakes and turtles, go on a leisurely hike through the Center's wilderness preserve.
Time: Apr.-Oct., Tues.-Sat., 8:30 a.m.-4:30 p.m.; Sun., 2-5 p.m. rest of year, Tues.-Sat., 9 a.m.-5 p.m.
Place: 2.5 mi. W of town on CT 202.
Contact: (203) 567-0015

Exotic Gardens

White Glower Farm is noted for its acres of exotic gardens, but particularly for tuberous begonias. Displays are best in mid- to late-summer.
Time: Apr.-Oct., Wed.-Mon., 9 a.m.-4:30 p.m.
Place: 3 mi. S of town on CT 63.
Contact: (203) 567-0801

Manchester

"Do Touch" Museum

Exhibits change frequently at the Lutz Children's Museum, but always include a wise old owl, a stamp printing exhibit, medical tools and many others. Kids are encouraged to participate in many of the displays.
Time: Sept.-July, Tues.-Sun., 2-5 p.m.
Place: 126 Cedar St.
Contact: (203) 643-0949

Meriden

Picnic Spot

On a clear day in Hubbard Park you can see from Massachusetts to Long Island Sound. The crenelated Castle Craig serves as a stone observation tower.
Time: Mon.-Fri., sunrise to sunset (closed weekends to non-residents).
Place: Hubbard Park, on W. Main St.
Contact: (203) 634-0003, ext. 410

Pewter

The Heritage House recreates a typical Georgian dining room, silversmith shop, pewterer's workshop and tavern scene in a replica of New England life 200 years ago. While pewter and silver are on sale, there's no charge to look.
Time: Mon.-Sat., 10:30 a.m.-3 p.m.
Place: 500 S. Broad St.
Contact: (203) 634-2541

Middletown

Theory of Relativity

Here's a shrine for space-age scientists. The original manuscripts of Albert Einstein's Theory of Relativity are

kept in the Science Library of Wesleyan University.
Time: May-Sept., 7 a.m.-8 p.m.; Sept.-May, Sun.-Thurs., 7 a.m.-2 a.m.; Fri.-Sat., 7 a.m.-midnight.
Place: Wesleyan University, Science Library.
Contact: (203) 347-9411, ext. 296

16,000 Prints

Thousands of prints, many of them by master artists, are represented in the Davidson Art Center. Its collection spans the years from 1420 to the present.
Time: Mon.-Fri., noon-4 p.m.; Sat.-Sun., 2-5 p.m.

Place: Wesleyan University, on High St.
Contact: (203) 347-9411

Milford

Oyster Festival

Band music, street dancing, parades, clowns and about 50,000 people each year pack into Milford for the Oyster Festival. It's a slightly misleading name since the lowly creature has mostly disappeared from the area, but it's still a festive time.
Time: Mid-Aug.
Place: Milford Center.
Contact: (203) 878-0681

Mohegan

Indian Museum

The Indian-owned and operated Tantaquidgeon Lodge Indian Museum features works by New England tribes. Outside are replicas of dwellings used by regional Indians, including a wigwam and log house.
Time: May-Oct., 10 a.m.-6 p.m.
Place: On CT 32, in town.
Contact: (203) 848-9145

Naugatuck

Ummm, Boy!

Peter Paul offers tours of its plant where Mounds and

Almond Joys are made. Tours last 30 minutes and end with a free candy bar and a York Mint.
Time: Mon.-Wed., 10:30 a.m. and 1:30 p.m., by appt.
Place: On CT 63, in town.
Contact: (203) 729-0221, ext. 271
Note: No cameras allowed. No children under 6.

New Britain

Kids' Delight

The New Britain Youth Museum is custom-made for kids. It has hands-on displays, live fish, boas, a monkey, horned reptiles and an outstanding collection of circus memorabilia.
Time: Mon.-Fri., 1-5 p.m.; Sat., 10 a.m.-4 p.m.; Sun., 2-5 p.m.
Place: 30 High St.
Contact: (203) 225-3020

Hudson River School

About 500 of the 4,000 works owned by the New Britain Museum of American Art are on display at one time. Most popular are the works representing the Hudson River school.
Time: Tues.-Sun., 1-5 p.m.
Place: 56 Lexington St.
Contact: (203) 229-0257

CONNECTICUT

New Haven

Powder House Day

There's nothing traitorous about it. New Haven's the only city in the US to celebrate the courage of Benedict Arnold. Men in full Revolutionary War garb reenact his taking of the local Powder House.
Time: 1st Sat. in May.
Place: New Haven Green.
Contact: (203) 787-6735

Free Concerts

The city of New Haven offers several free musical events throughout the year. Most of the concerts are family-oriented, and some of them are given in neighborhood locations. Check with the contact for a list of the events scheduled currently.
Time: July-Aug., Wed. noon; Wed. evening.
Place: The Green.
Contact: (203) 727-1000

70-Foot Brontosaurus

Free only three days of the week, the Peabody Museum of Natural History is well-known for its dinosaur skeletons—especially the enormous 70-foot brontosaurus!
Time: Free Mon., Wed., Fri. only, 9 a.m.-5 p.m.
Place: 170 Whitney Ave., at Sachem St., on Yale campus.
Contact: (203) 436-0850

Art Gallery

The Yale University Art Gallery, the oldest college art museum in the US, stands out in 19th- and 20th-century works, particularly those by American artists.
Time: Tues.-Sat., 10 a.m.-5 p.m. (Thurs., 6-9 p.m. during school year); Sun., 2-5 p.m.
Place: 1111 Chapel St.
Contact: (203) 436-0574

Yale Campus Tours

One-hour tours of the Yale campus give a brief history of the school and background on the campus. Guides are provided free of charge as a service to visitors of this world-famous university.
Time: Tours: Mon.-Fri., 10:30 a.m. and 2 p.m.; Sat.-Sun., 1:30 p.m.
Place: 344 College St.
Contact: (203) 436-8330

British Art

The Yale Center for British Art covers nearly everything from the Elizabethan period to the mid-19th century. Its collection is extraordinary, with paintings, drawings, prints, sculptures and rare books.
Time: Tues.-Sat., 10 a.m.-5 p.m.; Sun., 2-5 p.m.
Place: 1080 Chapel St.
Contact: (203) 432-4594

Gravestone Rubbings

Many famous people (such as Noah Webster and Eli Whitney) were buried in Grove St. Cemetery. The tombstones of patriots and prominent historical figures make this a fine place for gravestone rubbings.
Place: 227 Grove St., near Yale campus.
Contact: (203) 787-1443

Patent Models

The patent model for Eli Whitney's cotton gin and other 19th-century inventions are found in the New Haven Colony Historical Society. Its exhibits change every four months.
Time: Tues.-Fri., 10 a.m.-5 p.m.; Sat.-Sun., 2-5 p.m.
Place: 114 Whitney Ave.
Contact: (203) 562-4183

Newington

Hams' Haven

The American Radio Relay League offers tours of exhibits on amateur radio communications. And it sets up an Amateur Radio Field Day Contest on the third weekend of June each year; more than 1,500 groups compete in the contest, at various locations through-out the country.

Time: Tours: Mon.-Fri., on the hour except noon, 9 a.m.-4 p.m.

Place: 225 Main St.

Contact: (203) 666-1541

New London

Small Zoo

The zoo at the Hubert F. Moran Nature Center is small but good. Kids will enjoy the monkeys, goats and baby animals. The park is a pleasant place for a picnic as well.

Time: June-Sept., noon-5 p.m.

Place: Chester St.

Contact: (203) 443-2865, ext. 254

US Coast Guard Academy

Tour the *Eagle*, a ship used to train in cadets on summer cruises; watch a 20-minute slide and film presentation; visit the museum to see its many ship models; and see dress parades at the US Coast Guard Academy!

Time: Visitor's pavilion: mid-May-Aug., 9 a.m.-5 p.m. Museum: Fri., 9 a.m.-4:30 p.m. Parades: Apr.-May, Sept.-Oct., Fri., 4 p.m. *Eagle:* Apr.-May, Sept.-Oct., please call ahead for times.

Place: Off I-95 on CT 32.

Contact: (203) 444-8444

Dollhouse Collection

The Lyman Allyn Museum is small but superb. Its outstanding feature is a collection of

dolls, toys and dollhouses. The latter includes a 20-room model with three levels furnished in minute detail. The museum is most impressive in December when laid out as a country store. A gem.

Time: Tues.-Sat., 1-5 p.m.; Sun., 2-5 p.m.

Place: 625 Williams St.

Contact: (203) 443-2545

Bee Hive

An active bee hive, crabs, fish and other live animals high-light the Thames Science Center.

Time: Mon.-Sat., 9 a.m.-5 p.m.; Sun., noon-4 p.m.

Place: Gallows Ln., on Connecticut College campus.

Contact: (203) 442-0391

Norwich

Gallery of Casts

Most unique at the Slater Museum is its cast gallery, where you'll find *copies* of 50 major pieces of sculpture. The museum sponsors changing exhibits throughout the year, although it does have a small permanent collection of Oriental and American pieces.

Time: June-Aug., Tues.-Sun., 1-4 p.m. Rest of year, Mon.-Fri., 9 a.m.-4 p.m.; Sat.-Sun., 1-4 p.m.

Place: 108 Crescent St., campus of Norwich Free Academy.

Contact: (203) 887-2506

Old Lyme

Artistic Paint Job

Painters lived in the Florence Griswold House, which is unique in that the walls and door panels have become "canvas" for artistic creations. Throughout the home are works of American impression-

CONNECTICUT

Old Lyme

ist painters as well as decorative and historical objects.

Time: June-Aug., Tues.-Sat., 10 a.m.-5 p.m.; Sept.-May, Wed.-Fri. and Sun., 1-5 p.m.
Place: 96 Lyme St.
Contact: (203) 434-5542

Rocky Hill

Dinosaur Prints

In 1960 over 500 dinosaur footprints were discovered in what is now Dinosaur State Park. The state built a geodesic dome over the prints to protect them. Kids are encouraged to make their own dinosaur prints in cement provided for that purpose!

Time: 9 a.m.-4 p.m.
Place: West St.
Contact: (203) 566-2304

Waterbury

Calder Original Models

The models that Alexander Calder used to make two of his famous pieces can be seen at Segre's Iron Works. An offbeat attraction, but one which shows a glimpse of the development of his art.

Time: Always on view.
Place: 116 Reidville Dr.
Contact: (203) 753-2707

West Cornwall

Covered Bridge

This state can claim many lovely covered bridges. But the bridge that spans the Housatonic River at West Cornwall is one of the most photogenic sites in the state.

Place: On CT 128.
Contact: (203) 566-2410

Statewide

Free Parks

Of the 88 Connecticut state parks, only 18 charge entrance fees. If you'd like information on the park system, write or call the contact below.

Contact: Office of Parks and Recreation, Room 265, State Office Bldg., Hartford, CT 06115; (203) 566-2304.

Scenic Drives

US 1 along the shore and US 7 north from Norwalk to the state line are two of the more scenic routes in a state noted for its natural beauty. The Norwalk route is best in the fall.

DELAWARE

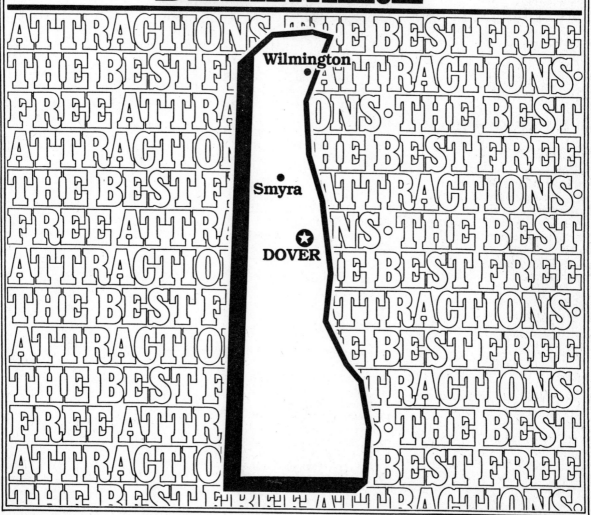

Wilmington

Smyra

★ DOVER

DELAWARE

Angola

St. George's Chapel

This Georgian church, built in 1794, is noted for its lovely woodwork—worth seeing if you're in the area.
Place: On DE 285.
Contact: (302) 945-1833

Bethany Beach

Safe Beach

Bethany Beach offers miles of public and state-owned beaches, suited to families looking for safe swimming areas free of charge. Dance troupes perform during the summer in this area.
Contact: (302) 539-8129
Note: Beach is dry—no alcohol allowed.

Claymont

Historic Home

The Robinson House served as a private residence through the 18th and 19th centuries. George Washington was one of the home's most notable guests. A good part of the original woodwork and fireplaces have been preserved.
Time: Sun., 1:30-4:30 p.m.
Place: NW corner of Rte. 92 (Naaman's Rd.) and Rte. 13 (Philadelphia Pike).
Contact: (302) 798-4897

Cowgill's Corner

Octagonal Schoolhouse

Here you'll find one of the earliest one-room schools in the state, dating back to 1836. It was built in its unusual octagonal shape to provide more space and light. The interior reflects school life of the 19th century. There's also an interesting collection of textbooks from 1800 to 1920.
Time: Sat., 10 a.m.-4:30 p.m.; Sun., 1:30-4:30 p.m.
Place: Just N of town, off DE 9.
Contact: (302) 736-4266

Dagsboro

Prince George's Chapel

Built in 1757, Prince George's Chapel still has its original unpainted pine interior. A worthwhile stop if you're in the area.
Time: Sat., 10 a.m.-4:30 p.m.; Sun., 1:30-4:30 p.m.
Place: Off DE 26.
Contact: (302) 645-9318

Delmar

Mason-Dixon Line

The Mason-Dixon monument marks the historic Mason-Dixon line, and families have a good time photographing each other at this spot. The monument was erected in 1768 to distinguish the boundaries between the Calvert and Penn families.
Place: W of town on DE 54.
Contact: (302) 846-2664

The "Highball" Signal

Here you'll view an original railroad pulley, which raises and lowers a large white ball to indicate the condition of the track ahead. The signal was first put to use in 1832 and was the last in use on the Pennsylvania line. A 1929 caboose is the setting for the railroad museum.
Time: Museum: Mon.-Fri., 9 a.m.-3 p.m.; weekends, by appt.
Place: Pennsylvania Ave. W.
Contact: (302) 846-2664

Dover

Old Country Store

The McDowell-Collins Country Store House is a mercantile museum laid out as it might have been at the turn of the century. Here you can also pick up a free brochure on the Dover Heritage Trail.
Time: Mon.-Fri., 10 a.m.-2 p.m.
Place: 408 S. State St.
Contact: (302) 678-2040

State House

The State House, the second oldest in the country, has been restored to its 1793 appearance. Guided tours begin from the Margaret O'Neill Information Center.
Time: Tues.-Sat., 10 a.m.-4:30 p.m.; Sun., 1:30-4:30 p.m.
Place: The Green.
Contact: (302) 736-4266

Apollo Space Suits

The Delaware State Museum is a beautiful building dating

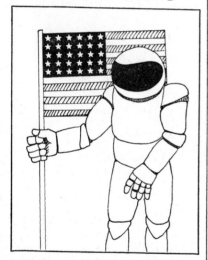

back to 1790. Inside are exhibits from the early 17th century to the space age. Most popular are the Apollo space suits and the Victor Talking Machine models!
Time: Tues.-Sat., 10 a.m.-4:30 p.m.; Sun., 1:30-4:30 p.m.
Place: 316 S. Governor's Ave.
Contact: (302) 674-8818

Colonial Home

The John Dickinson Mansion is an elegant old home with great historic appeal. Built in 1740, it is furnished in 18th-century antiques and overlooks a formal English garden.
Time: Tues.-Sat., 10 a.m.-5 p.m.; Sun., 1-5 p.m.
Place: Off DE 113 on Kitts Hummock Rd. (S end of Dover Air Force Base).
Contact: (302) 734-9439

Johnson Memorial

Delaware's Johnson Memorial is a tribute to the man who founded the Victor Talking Machine Company, known today as RCA. Here you'll find victrolas, recordings (one of Enrico Caruso), and a painting of "Nipper"—the dog who is the famous RCA trademark.
Time: Tues.-Sat., 10 a.m.-4:30 p.m.; Sun., 1:30-4:30 p.m.
Place: 316 S. Governor's Ave.
Contact: (302) 674-8818

Governor's House

Known locally as Woodburn, the governor's residence was built in 1790 and is one of the finest examples of Georgian architecture in the state. It also has a colorful history, having served as part of the underground railroad in pre-Civil War days.
Time: Sat., 2:30-4:30 p.m.
Place: King's Hwy., S of Division St.
Contact: (302) 736-5656

Historic Walking Tour

Take the time to follow the Dover Heritage Trail. It will lead you to many of the city's most interesting historical buildings and sights. Pick up a free brochure from the Delaware State Visitors Service.
Place: Delaware State Visitors Service, 630 State College Rd.
Contact: (302) 736-4266

Frankford

Bald Cypress Stand

The Great Cypress Swamp has the northernmost stand of bald cypress in the US. Worth a stop if you're in the area.
Place: S on US 113, then W on DE 54. Watch for signs.
Contact: (302) 875-5153

Frederica

Barratt's Chapel

Built in 1780, Barratt's Chapel is known as "The Cradle of

DELAWARE

Frederica

Methodism in America." The interior is much as it was 200 years ago.
Time: Tues.-Sat., 9:30 a.m.-4:30 p.m.; Sun., 1-5 p.m. Evening services: summer, Sun., 7:30 p.m.
Place: 1 mi. N of town on US 113.
Contact: (302) 335-5544

Laurel

Cable-Drawn Ferry

The Woodland Ferry is one of the last cable-drawn ferries in the US. It can carry three cars at one time and has been in operation since 1793. While you cross the Nanticoke River (a five-minute ride), you'll pass heavily wooded land with lots of wildlife on shore. There's no charge!
Time: Sunrise to sunset.
Place: Across the Nanticoke River, 5 mi. NW of town on DE 78.
Contact: (302) 629-7742

Leipsic

Bombay Hook National Wildlife Refuge

This coastal wildlife refuge is one of the best in the state. It covers thousands of acres, most of which are brackish tidal marsh. There are auto tour routes, observation towers and a boardwalk. Fall migrations of Canada geese number more than 20,000 birds. Three hundred species have been sighted throughout the years, making this a birdwatchers' and photographers' haven.
Time: Sunrise to sunset.
Place: 2 mi. N of town on DE 9, then 2.5 mi. E.
Contact: (302) 653-9345

Qwaanendael Museum

This museum, built in 1931, is a replica of the Town Hall in Hoorn, Holland. Erected in honor of the 17th-century Dutch settlement, it seems strangely out of place in its American setting. Inside are maritime and military displays.
Time: Tues.-Sat., 10 a.m.-4:30 p.m.; Sun., 1:30-4:30 p.m.
Place: Savannah Rd. Kings Highway.
Contact: (302) 645-9418

Milford

Maritime Memorabilia

At North Bowers Beach make a short stop to see the maritime exhibits in the Bowers Beach Maritime Museum—another small, but good place to visit.
Time: May-Sept., Sat.-Sun., 11 a.m.-4 p.m.
Place: Main and Williams Sts.
Contact: (302) 335-5417

Ice Cream Social

Visit the Parson Thorne Mansion (named for a famous local citizen) on Parson Thorne Day—the festival's a delight. The grounds are the site of an old-fashioned ice cream social with many costumed citizens. You'll see craft and food booths galore.
Time: 2nd weekend in July. Call contact for exact date and times.
Contact: (302) 422-3301

Milton

History of Boat Building

The Lydia Ann B. Cannon Museum is small, but good. Exhibits are devoted to the history of boat building in the 1800s.
Time: Sat.-Sun., 2-4 p.m.
Place: 210-212 Union St.
Contact: (302) 684-4110

Newark

Hale Byrnes House

Washington met with his officers in the Hale Byrnes House

before the battle of Brandy-wine in 1777. This handsome brick structure was built in 1750. The period furnishings are of special interest.
Time: By appt. only.
Place: At jct. of DE 4 and 7.
Contact: (302) 994-1777

Mineral Room

The University of Delaware's Du Pont Mineral Room offers an exceptional collection of rocks and minerals. Kids will love it.
Time: By appt.
Place: Penny Hall, Academy St.
Contact: (302) 738-2569

New Castle

19th-Century Mansion

Buena Vista, built in 1845-47 for Senator John M. Clayton, is furnished with period pieces and decorated with works of art from the State Collections. The home serves as a state conference and reception center, but is open for tours.
Time: Sat., 10 a.m.-4:30 p.m., or by appt.
Place: On DE 13, SW of New Castle.
Contact: (302) 571-3056

New Castle Heritage Trail

Follow the New Castle Heritage Trail, a five-block walking tour in one of Delaware's most historical areas—not to be missed. The walking tour will take you to The Strand, The Green and several historical buildings. The trail ends in a park on the Delaware River. You can get a brochure about the trail from the contact below.
Contact: Bureau of Travel Development, 45 on The Green, Dover, DE 19901; (302) 736-4254.

Old Court House

The Old Court House was the colonial capitol and a county seat for years. Built in 1732, it was restored in 1801 and contains authentic furnishings. Of special interest is the raised judge's bench in the courtroom.
Time: April-Oct., Tues.-Sat., 10 a.m.-4:30 p.m.; Sun., 1:30-4:30 p.m. Rest of year, Tues.-Sat., 11 a.m.-4 p.m.; Sun. , 1-4 p.m.
Place: Delaware St.
Contact: (302) 571-3059

Rehoboth Beach

Boardwalk

The popular bandstand by the waters of Rehoboth Beach hosts a series of free events throughout much of the summer. For a list, write the contact below.
Contact: Rehoboth Beach Chamber of Commerce, 73 Rehoboth Ave., Rehoboth Beach, DE 19971; (302) 227-2233.

Body Surfing

The renowned Rehoboth Beach appeals not only to fami-

lies but also to body surfers who, with extended arms, ride the heavy waves into shore.
Contact: (302) 227-2233

DELAWARE

Smyrna

Queen Anne Country House

The Allee House, built in 1753, is one of the state's better examples of the Queen Anne style. Stop in and view the interior, furnished in period pieces.

Time: Sat.-Sun., 1:30-4:30 p.m.
Place: Dutch Neck Rd., off DE 9, E of town.
Contact: (302) 736-4266

The Lindens

This is part of the Duck Creek Village, built in 1700, and served as a miller's house before 1765. Several buildings in this historic site can be seen.

Time: 10 a.m.-4:30 p.m.
Place: 1.5 mi. NW of town on DE 6.
Contact: (302) 653-5419

South Bowers

Archaeological Museum

Each summer you can see the excavations at Island Field near South Bowers Beach. The museum here was built over a prehistoric Indian cemetery and features Indian relics. Children's programs are fea-

tured on Tuesdays (call for current information). Slide presentation too.

Time: March-Nov., Tues.-Sat., 10 a.m.-4:30 p.m.; Sun., 1:30-4:30 p.m.
Place: South Bowers Beach, off DE 113.
Contact: Office of the Director, Division of Historical and Cultural Affairs, Hall of Records, Dover, DE 19901; (302) 736-4651.

Wilmington

Brandywine Zoo

Here's a change of pace for the kids—a zoo (including a good children's zoo) and a park for a quiet picnic.

Time: 10 a.m.-4 p.m.
Place: N. Park Dr.
Contact: (302) 571-7747

Lincoln Collection

Over 2,000 books, photographs and pamphlets make up the noted Lincoln Collection which depicts Lincoln's private and public lives.

Time: By appt.
Place: University of Delaware Goodstay Center, 2600 Pennsylvania Ave.
Contact: (302) 654-3123

Old Swedes' Church

Built in 1698, this stark stone church is the oldest standing original church in Wilmington.

It is still used for religious services. Visit also the nearby Hendrickson House Museum (1690).

Time: Mon.-Sat., noon-4 p.m.
Place: 606 Church St.
Contact: (302) 652-5629

Restored Jail

Lock yourself up in the restored jail in the basement of the Old Town Hall. Before doing so, view the exhibits of silver, furniture and decorative arts.

Time: Tues.-Fri., noon-4 p.m.; Sat., 10 a.m.-4 p.m.
Place: 512 Market St.
Contact: (302) 655-7221

Port Tours

Tours of the port last 90 minutes and take you by huge warehouses and giant cranes that lift all kinds of wares onto ships in the dock area. There are often tours of the ships themselves; ask your guide if a ship tour is available.

Time: Mon.-Fri., 8 a.m.-noon and 1-4 p.m.
Place: Port Office, at the foot of Christiana Ave.
Contact: (302) 571-4600

Tour Historic Wilmington

Six walking and driving tours take you to many of Wilmington's free historic sights. Pick up a brochure at the contact below. One tour near the contact leads you through Wilmington Square, an historic group of six 18th-century houses.

Time: Tour of Wilmington Square by appt.
Place: Brochure: 505 Market St.
Square: 500 Market St. Mall.
Contact: Brochure and square: (302) 655-7161.

Statewide

Fishing for Free

Surf casting and recreational shell fishing along Delaware's generous shoreline do not require a license. However, you must take crabs and clams only in designated areas. For more information write or call the contact below.

Contact: Delaware State Travel Service, 630 State College Rd., Dover, DE 19901; (302) 736-4254.

Scenic Auto Route

If you're not in a hurry, get off the super highways and drive along DE 9 which will bring you closer to the coast—a far more enjoyable and scenic route!

Contact: (302) 736-4254

DISTRICT OF COLUMBIA

⭐ US CAPITOL

DISTRICT OF COLUMBIA

1876 Remembered

The Arts and Industries Building recreates the feeling of the late 19th century by displaying exhibits of the 1876 Philadelphia Centennial Exposition.
Time: 10 a.m.-5:30 p.m.
Place: Ninth and Jefferson Dr. SW.
Contact: (202) 357-2700

Band Concerts

Held in numerous places throughout the city, band concerts are under park service supervision. Call the contact for up-to-date schedules.
Time: June-Aug., normally in early evening.
Place: Varying locations.
Contact: (202) 426-6700

Money by the Millions

At the Bureau of Engraving and Printing tour tickets are issued on a first-come, first-serve basis during the peak tourist season. Here you'll see millions of dollars and lovely stamps printed. Each dollar has to be replaced every 18 months—one reason the presses are almost always rolling!
Time: Mon.-Fri., 8 a.m.-2 p.m.
Place: 14th and C Sts. SW.
Contact: (202) 447-9709

Cherry Blossom Festival

In April the Japanese cherry trees burst into bloom around the Jefferson Memorial, Tidal Basin and Washington Monument. For one week the city celebrates with many festivities, including a parade with national high school and collegiate bands.
Contact: (202) 789-7000

Senate Action

Write your congressman and ask for a free visitor's pass which allows you to visit Congress and sit in on Senate and House sessions. The action is rarely fast, but interesting for the first-time visitor!
Note: You'll need your representative's name. Then write the Honorable ——————, House of Representatives (or US Senate), Washington, DC 20515.

Peaceful Pace

Constitution Gardens and the Lincoln Memorial Reflecting Pool provide a relaxing oasis and needed change of pace from non-stop sightseeing. You can visit the small island in the center of the 6-acre lake by taking the footbridge.
Place: Between Washington Monument and Lincoln Memorial.

Dollar Bill Portrait

The Corcoran Gallery of Art is strong both in American portraits, including Stuart's $1 bill rendition of Washington, and in paintings of the Hudson River school. The gallery is the oldest and largest private art museum in the city.
Time: Tues.-Sun., 10 a.m.-4:30 p.m.; Thurs., 10 a.m.-9 p.m.
Place: 17th St. and New York Ave. NW.
Contact: (202) 638-3211

Lovely Home

Dumbarton Oaks, a magnificent home and birthplace of the United Nations, boasts a glass-domed museum with a fine collection of jade, textiles and jewelry.
Time: 2-4:45 p.m.
Place: 1703 32nd St. NW.
Contact: (202) 342-3200

Stunning Garden

Surrounding the mansion is Dumbarton Oaks Garden, which is formal in style and covers 27 acres on a terraced hillside. The classic garden is an important stop for anyone with a botanic bent.
Time: 2-4:45 p.m.
Place: 1703 32nd St. NW.
Contact: (202) 342-3200

Embassy Row

A delightful walk—amble along Massachusetts Avenue and see the names of many embassies clearly marked.

Blazing Barrels

One-hour guided tours give a brief background on the Federal Bureau of Investigation. Tours include a firearms demonstrazion—spent shells are given out as souvenirs.
Time: Mon.-Fri., 9 a.m.-4:15 p.m.
Place: Ninth and Pennsylvania Ave. NW.
Contact: (202) 324-3447

Fireworks

As many as 250,000 people attend the 20-minute fireworks show at dark each year to celebrate our country's independence. Quite a spectacle on the Washington Monument grounds.
Time: July 4th.
Place: Washington Monument.
Contact: (202) 426-6700

Renaissance Books

The famed Folger Shakespeare Library contains a superb collection of Renaissance books and magazines, a replica of an Elizabethan theatre and a scale model of the Globe Playhouse.
Time: Mon.-Sat., 11 a.m., noon and 1 p.m.
Place: 201 E. Capitol St. SE.
Contact: (202) 544-4600

Lincoln Artifacts

At Ford's Theatre, still used for theatre performances, you'll find a museum containing personal artifacts of President Lincoln.
Time: 9 a.m.-5 p.m.
Place: 511 Tenth St. NW.
Contact: (202) 426-6924
Note: Theatre performances are not free.

Catacombs

During your tour of the Franciscan Monastery you'll be transported back to the Middle Ages. The 45-minute tour leads you into catacombs and replicas of Holy Land shrines.
Time: 8:30 a.m.-4 p.m.; please call in advance.
Place: 14th and Quincy Sts. NE.
Contact: (202) 526-6800

Restored Home

Visit the restored Frederick Douglas Memorial Home, dedicated to the black educator who was a close friend of Abraham Lincoln.
Time: Apr.-Aug., 9 a.m.-5 p.m.; rest of year, 9 a.m.-4 p.m.
Place: 1411 W St. SE.
Contact: (202) 889-1736

Freebies

Check "This Week in Washington" in the *Washington Post* on Thursday and "Calendar" in the *Washington Star* on Friday for current listings of free films, lectures, concerts and special events!

Oriental Collection

The Freer Gallery of Art is known primarily for its exquisite array of Near and Far Eastern art objects. It also has a collection of works by James McNeill Whistler.
Time: 10 a.m.-5:30 p.m.
Place: 12th and Jefferson Dr. SW.
Contact: (202) 357-2700

Frisbee Festival

Learn a few tricks and get into the amateur action during the

Frisbee Festival, sponsored by the National Air and Space Museum!
Time: Early Sept.
Place: Mall grounds.
Contact: (202) 789-7000

Free Tourist Information

Stop off at the Gateway Tour Center for free information, maps, and a shuttle to the Air and Space Museum. Note that there is a charge for the wax museum at this location.
Time: Mar.-Aug., 9 a.m.-9 p.m.; rest of year, 10 a.m.-7 p.m.
Place: Fourth and E. Sts. SW.
Contact: (202) 554-2604

Georgetown

Named after England's George II, historic Georgetown is one of the city's more chic and fashionable districts. Ideal for a walk which takes you past restored buildings, trendy boutiques, and "in" restaurants.
Place: W of Rock Creek Park.

Sunday Afternoon in Georgetown

Varying free events, including band and concert music, entertain visitors in historic Georgetown on most Sunday afternoons in the summer.

Check with the contact for scheduled programs.
Time: May-Sept., Sun., usually at 2 p.m.
Place: Georgetown, between 30th and Jefferson Sts.
Contact: (202) 789-7000

Noted Artists

Only a portion of the 6,000-plus works in the collection of the Hirshhorn Museum are on display at any one time, but these include brilliant paintings and sculptures by noted artists—not to be missed.
Time: 10 a.m.-5:30 p.m.
Place: Independence Ave. at Eighth St. SW.
Contact: (202) 381-6264

Mosque

The Islamic Center, the leading US mosque, is well worth a visit. The interior features elegant Iranian carpets and a pulpit of 100,000 pieces of wood assembled without nails or glue. An unusual side trip.
Time: 10 a.m.-4 p.m.
Place: 2551 Massachusetts Ave. NW.
Contact: (202) 332-3451

Jefferson Memorial

The Jefferson Memorial reflects the style popular with the third president of the United States. For two weeks in early April the surrounding cherry trees blossom, making this a highlight of the city at that time! A fitting tribute to the man who drafted the Declaration of Independence.
Place: S bank of the Tidal Basin.
Contact: (202) 426-6821

Free Concerts

John F. Kennedy Center for the Performing Arts takes out a half-page ad in the Sunday "Style" section of the *Washington Post* and in the "Arts and Books" section of the *Washington Star* to let people know what will be happening during the following week at the Center. The information number below should—but frequently does not—know what is going on! Be persistent.
Place: Rock Creek Pkwy. and New Hampshire Ave. NW.
Contact: (202) 254-3600

Jousting

Not the old-fashioned version, but a newer one which tests a rider's skill as he (or she) tries to spear suspended rings. Many of the riders are in their early teens!
Time: Oct.
Place: Washington Monument.
Contact: (202) 426-6700

Library of Congress

This is the world's largest library. On a free tour you'll see a rare Gutenberg Bible (1455), a draft of the Declaration of Independence in Jefferson's handwriting and drafts of Lincoln's Gettysburg Address.
Time: Mon.-Fri., 9 a.m.-4 p.m.
Place: 10 First St. SE.
Contact: (202) 287-5458

Calendar of Events

The Library of Congress sponsors many free events, including films. Pick up a "Calendar of Events" from the Information Desk.
Time: Mon.-Fri., 9 a.m.-4 p.m.
Place: 10 First St. SE.
Contact: (202) 287-5458

Lincoln Memorial

Fifty-six steps lead to the inner chamber of the Lincoln Memorial where Lincoln's brooding marble figure sits on a throne chair. Each step symbolizes one year in the emancipator's life.
Time: 8 a.m.-midnight.
Place: W. Potomac Park, 23rd St. NW.
Contact: (202) 426-6841

Looking Under Lincoln

Unusual tours, usually lasting an hour, are offered of the cave below the Lincoln Memorial. Guides explain how the caves were formed in the limestone and answer any questions you may have—all at no charge.
Time: By advance arrangement.
Place: Lincoln Memorial.
Contact: (202) 426-6895

Brass Rubbings

London Brass Rubbing Center features rubbings of old English church brasses as well as portraits of knights, ladies and merchants of medieval England. There's a fee only to make a rubbing—no charge to look.
Time: 9 a.m.-5 p.m.
Place: Washington Cathedral, Massachusetts and Woodley Aves. NW.
Contact: (202) 244-9328

Marines on Parade

Close-order marching and tricky bayonet handling draw respect from visitors watching the Silent Drill Team in action. Also inspiring are the parade and performances by the Marine Band and the Drum and Bugle Corps.
Time: June-Sept., Fri., 8 p.m.
Place: Marine Barracks, Eighth

and I Sts. SE.
Contact: (202) 433-4173

Free Films

Martin Luther King Memorial Library sponsors many free films, poetry readings and cultural events. Pick up a free calendar for up-to-date schedules.
Time: Mon.-Thurs., 9 a.m.-9 p.m.; Sat.-Sun., 9 a.m.-5:30 p.m. Call for summer hours.
Place: 901 G St. NW.
Contact: Events: (202) 727-1186; films: 727-1265.
Note: Limited free parking.

Meridian Hill Park

A charming place with cascading pools and sculptured

fountains—good for a break.
Place: 16th St. at Florida Ave.
NW.
Contact: (202) 426-6700

African Art

The Museum of African Art features a fascinating collection of sculpture, musical instruments and masks from over 20 African countries. The archives contain over 100,000 slides and photographs related to Africa and its cultures.
Time: Mon.-Fri., 11 a.m.-5 p.m.;
Sat.-Sun., noon-5 p.m.
Place: 316-332 A St. NE.
Contact: (202) 287-3490 or
547-6222

Museum of American History

A fascinating glimpse into America's past with everything from the Star-Spangled Banner (the original) to Lincoln's handball. Very popular is the First Ladies' Hall showing costumes worn by famous women set in period rooms. And there are show biz and ethnic rooms; bikes, cars, and carriages; and even a railway exhibit.
Time: 10 a.m.-5:30 p.m.
Place: 14th and Constitution Ave.
NW.
Contact: (202) 357-2700

American Ingenuity

The Museum of History and Technology honors American ingenuity with displays ranging from Washington's false teeth to exhibits on Edison's phonograph and his invention of the light bulb.
Time: 10 a.m.-5:30 p.m.
Place: 14th St. and Constitution
Ave. NW.
Contact: (202) 357-1300

Hope Diamond

At the Museum of Natural History there's always a crowd around the sapphire-blue Hope diamond, and there are dozens of exhibits which kids love. In the insect zoo you can touch the non-poisonous specimens and watch scorpions and tarantulas being fed (call for schedule). The museum also has a huge meteorite collection—the list goes on and on.
Time: 10 a.m.-5:30 p.m.
Place: Tenth and Consitution
Ave. NW.
Contact: (202) 357-2700

Planetarium Show

There's no charge to see the 30-minute planetarium show at the National Air and Space Museum on Thursday. The planetarium is quite small, so come early to get a place!
Time: Free Thurs. noon only.
Place: Seventh and Independ-

ence Ave. SW.
Contact: (202) 357-2700

Touch a Moon Rock

In the National Air and Space Museum you'll see an incredible collection outlining man's reach for the stars. Fighter planes from the turn of the century, Lindbergh's *Spirit of St. Louis*, Apollo artifacts and moon rocks you can touch—these just scratch the surface of this great museum.
Time: 10 a.m.-5:30 p.m.
Place: Seventh and Independ-
ence Ave. SW.
Contact: (202) 357-2700

Sharks

Did you know that you could see sharks swimming one block from a subway station in downtown Washington? That's the pitch of the National Aquarium, where you can see sharks and dozens of other exotic fish in illuminated tanks for free.
Time: 9 a.m.-5 p.m.
Place: Basement, Department of
Commerce, 14th St. and
Constitution Ave. NW.
Contact: (202) 377-2825

Declaration of Independence

The National Archives preserve historic documents—from the famous Declaration of Independence to the infamous

Nixon tapes. Enter the building through the world's largest brass doors and look at documents protected in helium-filled cases.

Time: Apr.-Aug., 10 a.m.-9 p.m.; rest of year, 10 a.m.-5 p.m.
Place: Eighth St. and Constitution Ave. NW.
Contact: (202) 523-3099

Pageant of Peace

The president lights the national Christmas tree, and during the following week the Ellipse and Mall grounds host choral groups at night. There's a log burning to warm your hands, and a petting zoo for the kids.

Time: Dec. 18-23.

Sunday Evening Concerts

The National Gallery of Art sponsors free Sunday evening concerts. Be sure to call ahead for schedules and times. All seats are on a first-come, first-served basis so arrive early.

Time: Sept.-May, Sun., 7 p.m.
Place: E. Garden Ct. of West Bldg., Sixth and Constitution Ave. NW.
Contact: (202) 737-4215

Leonardo de Vinci

The National Gallery of Art houses one of the most extensive and finest collections of Western art in the world, ranging from the 13th century to the present. It is the only American gallery to own a work by Leonardo da Vinci. Note that there are now two buildings comprising this world-famous gallery—the East and West buildings.

Time: Apr.-Labor Day, Mon.-Sat., 10 a.m.-9 p.m.; rest of year, Mon.-Sat., 10 a.m.-5 p.m.; Sun., noon-9 p.m.
Place: Sixth and Constitution Ave. NW.
Contact: (202) 737-4215

Travel Films

The National Geographic Society runs films continuously in its Explorers Hall. Generally, two films are scheduled each week, but the same film runs all day. Call for film titles.

Time: Mon.-Fri., 9 a.m.-6 p.m.; Sat., 9 a.m.-5 p.m.; Sun., 10 a.m.-5 p.m.
Place: 17th and M Sts. NW.
Contact: (202) 857-7588, 857-7000

Explorers Hall

At the National Geographic Society you can view exhibits on its sponsored expeditions. Included are photographs taken by some of the country's finest travel photographers and original material brought back from all over the world. The 11-foot, free-standing globe, which fascinates many, is said to be the largest of its kind.

Time: Mon.-Fri., 9 a.m.-6 p.m.; Sat., 9 a.m.-5 p.m.; Sun., 10 a.m.-5 p.m.
Place: 17th and M Sts. NW.
Contact: (202) 857-7588 or 857-7000

National Museum of American Arts

The museum represents art from George Washington to the present, and 90% of the collection is by American artists. Of the 25,000 works owned by the museum 1,000-1,200 are on display at any one time.

Time: 10 a.m.-5:30 p.m.
Place: Eighth and G Sts. NW.
Contact: (202) 357-2700

Great Americans

The National Portrait Gallery honors great Americans with a collection of superb portraits, painted from life when it was possible. It occupies a portion of the Patent Office Building.

Time: 10 a.m.-5:30 p.m.
Place: Eighth and F Sts. NW.
Contact: (202) 357-2700

1,000 Firearms

The National Rifle Association of America displays over 1,000 arms from ancient to modern times, including some used by Teddy Roosevelt.

Time: 10 a.m.-4 p.m.
Place: 1600 Rhode Island Ave.
Contact: (202) 828-6000

Largest Roman Catholic Church

The National Shrine of the Immaculate Conception, the largest Roman Catholic church in the US, offers free guided tours. It also has the largest collection of 20th-century mosaics in the world, including "The Descent of the Holy Spirit," made from 1,250,000 pieces of Venetian glass tile.

Time: 7 a.m.-6 p.m.
Place: Fourth and Michigan Ave. NE.
Contact: (202) 526-8300

Zoo

More than 2,000 animals can be seen at the National Zoological Park. Among the most popular are the rare white tigers and the giant pandas. The zoo also has a large aviary where birds can be viewed in free flight.

Time: Grounds: 6 a.m.-8 p.m.
Building: June-Aug., 9 a.m.-6:30 p.m.; rest of year, 9 a.m.-4:30 p.m.

Place: 3001 Connecticut Ave. NW.
Contact: (202) 673-4800
Note: Parking fee for cars.

Up Periscope!

The Naval Memorial Museum traces the history of the Navy from its beginning to the Space Age. It is especially popular with kids, who can play with the periscopes which overlook the river, and climb onto the anti-aircraft guns and eventually into the test model for the *Trieste*—the sub which has taken the deepest dive into the ocean.

Time: Mon.-Fri., 9 a.m.-4 p.m.; Sat.-Sun., 10 a.m.-5 p.m.
Place: Ninth and M Sts. (US Washington Navy Yard).
Contact: (202) 433-2651

Navy Yard Ceremonies

The evening pageant and parade at the Navy Yard includes the stirring performance of the Ceremonial Guard and Drill Team (rifles with fixed bayonets flipped over heads). Free, but make reservations well in advance.

Time: June-Aug., Wed., 8:45 p.m.
Place: Navy Yard, Ninth and M St. SE.
Contact: Public Affairs Office, Hqtrs., Naval District Washington, Washington Naval Yard, Washington, D.C. 20374; (202) 433-2218.

Haunted House

The Octagon House, a lovely 18th-century mansion, was President Madison's home from 1814-1815. Take a tour and climb the staircase rumored to be haunted by two women who died here.

Time: Tues.-Fri., 10 a.m.-4 p.m.; Sat.-Sun., 1-4 p.m.
Place: 1799 New York Ave., 18th and E Sts.
Contact: (202) 638-3105

Pre-Revolutionary House

The Old Stone House, built in 1765, has been authentically

furnished to represent the era when it was built, right down to 18th-century apple peelers and candle dippers.

Time: 9:30 a.m.-5 p.m.
Place: 3051 M St. NW.
Contact: (202) 426-6851

Flour Mill

A miller will show you how to grind wheat and corn into flour at the Peirce Mill, a 19th-century waterwheel grist mill with giant grindstones.

Time: Wed.-Sun., 9 a.m.-5 p.m.
Place: Tilden St. and Beach Dr. NW.
Contact: (202) 426-6908

Lincoln Died Here

Lincoln died in a tiny bedroom in the Peterson House after being shot by John Wilkes Booth in 1865. The home has been renovated and can be seen by appointment.

Time: May-Labor Day, 9 a.m.-5 p.m., by appt.
Place: 516 Tenth St. NW.
Contact: (202) 426-6830

Impressionist Paintings

The Phillips Collection, small but very fine, is shown in an elegant mansion. Of special interest are the French impressionist paintings which can be fully appreciated in this unhurried atmosphere.

Time: Tues.-Sat., 10 a.m.-5 p.m.; Sun., 2-7 p.m.
Place: 1600-1612 21st St. NW.
Contact: (202) 387-2151 or 387-0691

Piano Recitals

At the museum known as the Phillips Collection you can enjoy free piano recitals in an elegant, oak-panelled drawing room. Seats are given on a first-come, first-served basis so come early.

Time: Sept.-early June, Sun., 5 p.m.
Place: 1600-1612 21st St. NW.
Contact: (202) 387-2151 or 387-0691

Decorative Arts

The Renwick Gallery, only a short walk from the White House, is a showcase for design and the decorative arts. The building, dating from the Civil War era, is a notable example of the French Empire style.

Time: 10 a.m.-5:30 p.m.
Place: 17th St. and Pennsylvania Ave. NW.
Contact: (202) 381-5811 or 381-6264

Join the Action

Rock Creek Nature Center draws visitors into the action with push-button quizzes and do-it-yourself devices. There's even a "bee city" and free planetarium shows.

Time: Tues.-Sat., 9:30 a.m.-5 p.m.
Place: 5200 Glover Rd. NW.
Contact: (202) 426-6829

Biking Trail

Either bike or hike the 8-mile trail through Rock Creek Park for a delightful outing. It runs partially through woods and nearly parallel to Rock Creek from the Maryland-DC line to the Kennedy Center.

Contact: (202) 426-6833

Cathedral Tour

Take a Sunday afternoon tour of St. Matthew's Cathedral—

one of the most impressive churches in the city.
Time: Tours: Sun., 2:30 and 4:30 p.m. Other times by appt.
Place: 1725 Rhode Island Ave. NW.
Contact: (202) 347-3215

Black Artists

The Smith-Mason Gallery is known for its contemporary paintings, prints and sculptures. Many of these are by black artists.
Time: Tues.-Fri., 1-4 p.m.; Sat., 10 a.m.-4 p.m.; Sun., 2-5 p.m.
Place: 1207 Rhode Island Ave. NW.
Contact: (202) 462-6323

Red Castle

The Smithsonian Building is the world-famous red "Castle on the Mall." The multi-turreted building is one of the best Gothic Revival buildings in the US. Here you'll find the information center for the many museums under the Smithsonian's jurisdiction. Ask for free brochures.
Time: 10 a.m.-5:30 p.m.
Place: 1000 Jefferson Dr.
Contact: (202) 357-2700

Supreme Court

When the Court is not in session, you can get a brief look at the inner workings of the nation's highest judicial body through guided tours.
Time: Tours: Mon.-Fri., 9:30 a.m.-3:30 p.m.
Place: First St. and Maryland Ave. NW.
Contact: (202) 252-3200

Rare Rugs

Rare rugs and an incredible collection of thousands of textiles from throughout the world make the Textile Museum a popular attraction. Donations are suggested, but there is no set entry fee.
Time: Tues.-Sat., 10 a.m.-5 p.m.
Place: 2320 S St. NW.
Contact: (202) 667-0442

Nature Walks

A statue of Theodore Roosevelt stands in the Potomac River on an island which has been set aside as the Roosevelt Memorial. You reach the island by a bridge and can meet a ranger on weekends for a guided nature walk. Walks begin at the statue.
Time: Park: 9 a.m.-sunset. Walks: Sat.-Sun., 11 a.m. and 2 p.m.
Place: On Roosevelt Island.
Contact: (202) 557-3635

Counterfeit Currency

The Treasury Department Exhibit Hall features displays on legitimate and counterfeit currency as well as films on the IRS.
Time: Tues.-Sat., 9:30 a.m.-3:30 p.m.
Place: 15th and Pennsylvania Ave. NW.
Contact: (202) 566-5221

Navy Uniforms

Truxton-Decatur Naval Museum displays ship models, uniforms and weaponry used by the Navy, Coast Guard, Marines and Merchant Marines.
Time: 10 a.m.-4 p.m.
Place: 1610 H St. NW.
Contact: (202) 842-0050

Torchlight Tattoo

The US Army presents its Torchlight Tattoo pageant on Wednesday evenings during the summer. Participants are dressed in authentic reproductions of revolutionary war uniforms.
Time: Early June-mid-Aug., Wed., 8:30 p.m.
Place: Jefferson Memorial.
Contact: (202) 692-9788

Tropical Jungle

The US Botanic Garden sets the scene—tropical and subtropical zones where palms, tropical fruits and orchids thrive in a miniature rain forest.
Time: June-Aug., 9 a.m.-9 p.m.; rest of year, 9 a.m.-5 p.m.

Place: Maryland Ave., between First and Second Sts. SW.
Contact: (202) 225-7099

Capitol Tours

The US Capitol is quite probably the most famous building in the New World. It is located in the geographic center of the city and acts as its hub in all senses. Free 40-minute tours bring the building and its history to life.
Time: 9 a.m.-4:30 p.m.
Place: E end of Mall.
Contact: (202) 224-3121

Capitol Band

Listen to military bands strike up on the West Front steps of the US Capitol in the evening! All four services perform at varying times throughout the summer.
Time: Mon.-Wed., Fri., 7 p.m.
Place: West Front steps of US Capitol.
Contact: (202) 224-3121

Free Subway

Rub elbows with senators and congressmen on the free shuttle connecting the US Capitol and the new Senate Office Building.
Time: Whenever Congress is in session, 9 a.m.-5 p.m.

80,000 Azaleas

The US National Arboretum, a 445-acre botanist's paradise during the blooming season, is noted for its flowering shrubs such as azaleas, camellias, and magnolias. Other special attractions are the Japanese gardens, the bonsai collection and a lovely scented herb garden.
Time: Mon.-Fri., 8 a.m.-5 p.m.; Sat.-Sun., 10 a.m.-5 p.m.
Place: 24th and R St. NE.
Contact: (202) 472-9100

Star Gazing

If possible, try to visit the US Naval Observatory in the evening to look through a giant telescope so large it's housed in its own dome. The evening tours are very popular so call or write weeks in advance to make a reservation.
Time: Mon.-Fri., 12:30 a.m. and 2 p.m.; evenings by reservation.
Place: Massachusetts Ave. and 34th St. NW.
Contact: Superintendent, US Naval Observatory, 34th St. and Massachusetts Ave. NW, Washington, DC 20390; (202) 254-4533

Lollipop Concert

The lollipop concert, a special children's program, is performed by the US Navy Band at the Jefferson Memorial.
Time: Late Aug.
Place: Jefferson Memorial.
Contact: (202) 433-2394

Highest Point

Washington Cathedral rests on the highest point in the city and rivals Europe's great medieval churches. Contact the church for a schedule of organ recitals on its magnificent 10,000-pipe organ.
Time: Mon.-Fri., 10 a.m.-3:15 p.m. (closed during lunch); Sat., 12:15-2 p.m.
Place: Wisconsin, Massachusetts and Woodley Aves. NW.
Contact: (202) 537-6200

Breathtaking Views

If you climb the 898 steps to the top of the 550-foot high Washington Monument, the ride down comes free (costs a

dime to go up). The view from the city's most famous landmark is stupendous! It took 40 years to build this, the world's largest masonry structure.
Time: June-Aug., 8 a.m.-midnight; rest of year, 9 a.m.-5 p.m.
Place: On the Mall at 15th St. NW.

White House

Thomas Jefferson, the third president, was the first to live in the White House, more accurately known as the Executive Mansion. The building was burned by the British in 1814. White paint was used to cover the fire damage—thus the popular name. Free tickets (booth on the Ellipse) are required to enter.
Time: Tues.-Sat., 10 a.m.-noon.
Place: 1600 Pennsylvania Ave. NW.
Contact: (202) 456-7041

Easter Egg Roll

On the Monday after Easter children congregate on the White House lawn for the annual Easter egg roll—eggs are provided free!
Time: Mon. after Easter.
Place: White House lawn.
Contact: (202) 456-2323

White House Garden Tour

Each spring visitors are invited to a White House Garden tour. Dates vary according to the weather, but the tour is usually on a weekend in mid-April, and once again in the fall. Call for information. Note that no reservations or tickets are required. Simply show up and wait your turn in line.
Time: Mid-Apr. and fall weekends, 2-5 p.m.
Place: White House Gardens.
Contact: (202) 456-2323.

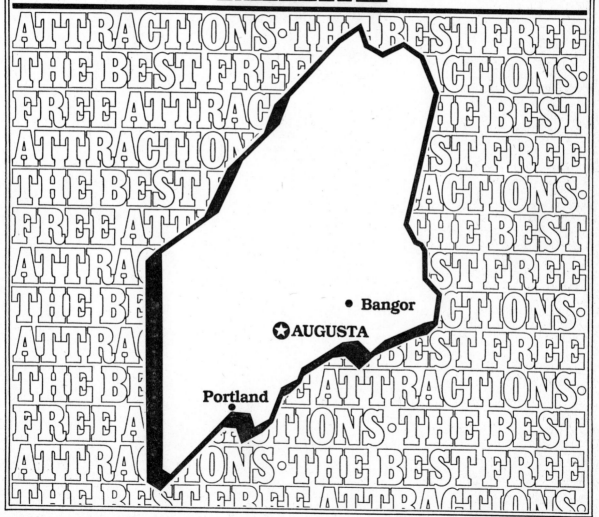

MAINE

MAINE

Andover

The Big Ear

A quiet valley provides a static-free sanctuary for the Andover Earth Station, a satellite control center for the Communications Satellite Corporation. Walk inside "The Big Bubble" globe that contains a 380-ton antenna called "The Big Ear." Tours begin with a 20-minute audio-visual program.
Time: Mem. Day-Labor Day, 9 a.m.-5 p.m.; rest of year, by appt.
Place: On ME 120.
Contact: (207) 364-7871

Augusta

Executive Mansion

James G. Blaine willed this 28-room mansion to the State, which has made it the official Governor's Residence. Tours, which last 30 minutes, are given in the afternoon only.
Time: Tours: Mon.-Fri., 2-3:30 p.m., on the half hour.
Place: State and Capitol Sts.
Contact: (207) 289-3771

Maine in a Nutshell

If it has to do with Maine, you'll probably find it in an exhibit at the Maine State Museum. The place has nearly everything, from live trout in a pool to Indian artifacts and 19th-century American glass.
Time: Mon.-Fri., 9 a.m.-5 p.m.; Sat., 10 a.m.-4 p.m.; Sun., 1-4 p.m.
Place: State St.
Contact: (207) 289-2301

River View

From a majestic dome rising 185 feet above the State Capitol Building you'll get a commanding view of Capitol Park and the Kennebec River. On a typical tour you will also see the legislature in action when it's in session.
Time: Mon.-Fri., 9 a.m.-5 p.m.
Place: State and Capitol Sts.
Contact: (207) 289-3771

Bar Harbor

Oldest Eastern Park

Among Acadia National Park's many attractions are vertical cliffs; a picturesque, rocky coast; 500 species of wildflowers; and the East Coast's highest peak, Mt. Cadillac. (Bring binoculars in the spring to view the seal rookeries and bald eagle nests.) Also superb are 120 miles of hiking trails. The visitor center at Hulls Cove features a 20-minute film.
Time: Visitor center: May-mid-Oct., 8:30 a.m.-4:30 p.m. Film: June-Sept., 9 a.m.-4 p.m., on the hour.
Place: On Mt. Desert Island via ME 3.
Contact: Acadia National Park Superintendent, RFD 1, P.O. Box 1, Bar Harbor, ME 04609; (207) 288-3338.

Genetics Lab

The Jackson Laboratory is the largest mammalian genetics

research center in the world—and world-renowned! Scientists breed over three million mice a year here, monitoring one hundred mutant strains. The hour-long tour includes lectures and a film.
Time: Laboratory: June 13-Sept. 5. Lecture and film: Tues., Wed., and Fri., 3 p.m.

Place: .5 mi. S of town via ME 3 on Mount Desert Island.
Contact: (207) 288-3373

Boothbay

Sailing Ships

An incredible sight: a dozen windjammers sailing into port at the same time! Windjammer Days also features free band music, a pageant, a parade and street dancing. The event attracts 50,000 people each year.
Time: Windjammers: 3 p.m. on 2nd Wed. of July.
Place: Harbor area.
Contact: (207) 633-2353

Seals

The Fisheries Research Lab hosts two seals in the summer months. You can also check out five tanks of lobsters, crab and shellfish and the lab's own tidal pool.
Time: Mem. Day-Columbus Day, Mon.-Fri., 8 a.m.-5 p.m.; Sat.-Sun., 9 a.m.-5 p.m.
Place: 2 mi. S off ME 27, at W. Boothbay Harbor.
Contact: (207) 633-5572

Shutter Bug

During early August, boats participating in the annual Tuna Tournament arrive at the wharf. The hustle and bustle as tuna are unloaded is fascinating to watch, and will cer-

tainly appeal to camera bugs who may be lucky enough to snap a shot of a 1,000-pound trophy.
Time: Early Aug.
Place: Wharf on E side of Atlantic Ave.
Contact: (207) 633-5440

Brownville Junction

Maine's Grand Canyon

Right in the middle of nowhere is Maine's version of the Grand Canyon (Gulf Hagas), appealing to hikers and backpackers who typically delight in this remote wilderness setting. If possible, allow a full two weeks to explore the area fully.

Brunswick

Medals from the Middle Ages

The Bowdoin College Museum of Art features a collection started in 1811. It includes classical antiquities, Old Master prints and drawings, and a highly unusual set of medals and plaquettes from the 15th and 16th centuries. The museum also has a gallery of American colonial and federal portraits.
Time: July-Labor Day, Tues.-Sat., 10 a.m.-5 p.m., 7-8:30 p.m.;

Sun., 2-5 p.m. Rest of year, Tues.-Fri., 10 a.m.-4 p.m.; Sat., 10 a.m.-5 p.m.; Sun., 2-5 p.m.
Place: Walker Art Bldg.
Contact: (207) 725-8731

Polar Expedition

The Peary-MacMillan Arctic Museum presents the story of the two Bowdoin alumni who braved the first successful expedition to the North Pole. A sledge, photographs, heavy fur suits and Eskimo art are just some of the related displays.
Time: Tues.-Fri., 10 a.m.-4 p.m. (to 5 p.m. in summer); Sat., 10 a.m.-5 p.m.; Sun., 2-5 p.m.
Place: Hubbard Hall, Bowdoin College.
Contact: (207) 725-8731

Bryant Pond

Crank Calls

This scenic burg (ideal for a picnic getaway) is one of the last American towns with crank-operated telephones. The Bryant Pond Telephone Company offers tours year-round.
Time: Tours: by appt., 9 a.m.-5 p.m.
Place: Rumford Ave.
Contact: Call your local operator and ask to be connected with Bryant Pond 9911. (You can't dial it directly!)

MAINE

Calais

Woodcock Mating Dance

Of the 207 species of birds found in the Moosehorn National Wildlife Refuge, the woodcocks are the most memorable. Early spring observers can see the woodcock's ritual mating dance in remote clearings, usually at dawn and dusk. Other attractions include hiking on logging trails, picking blueberries, watching the highest tide fluctuation in the continental US and catching a glimpse of wildlife—from moose to harbor seals. The visitor center offers films and lectures from May through September.

Time: Visitor center: June-Labor Day, 9 a.m.-6:30 p.m.
Place: Visitor center: off US 1, 6 mi. S of town.
Contact: (207) 454-3521

Caribou

Butterfly Collection

The Nylander Museum, named after a Swedish naturalist, has displays of butterflies, shells and marine life. Cases and cases of butterflies represent insects from throughout the world while the shell and geological specimens come mostly from Canada and Maine.

Time: Mid-Mar.-mid-Dec., Mon.-Fri., 1-4 p.m.
Place: 393 Main St.
Contact: (207) 493-4474

Castine

Ship Tour

Castine, so well preserved that the entire town has been declared a National Historic Site, is home port for the *State of Maine*, the training ship for the Maine Maritime Academy. You can tour it whenever it's in port—usually from late summer to early spring.

Time: July-Apr., 9 a.m.-4 p.m.
Place: Sea St.
Contact: (207) 326-4311

Ellsworth

Birdsacre Sanctuary

A captain's daughter transformed the Stanwood Homestead into a 19th-century bird sanctuary that today attracts more than a hundred species of birds. The home is filled with pioneer memorabilia, mounted birds, nests and eggs. Birdsacre Sanctuary also has a medical center that cares for chirping convalescents.

Time: June-Sept., 10 a.m.-4 p.m.
Place: Bar Harbor Rd., 2 mi. S of town on ME 3.
Contact: (207) 667-8460

Kennebunk

Wedding Cake House

This bright yellow house, now world-famous, is a reminder of the scroll-saw era. According to legend, the lace-style decoration was added by a sea captain to placate his new bride. He was called away before his new bride could get her wedding cake.

Time: Private, viewed from outside only.
Place: Summer St. on ME 35.
Contact: (207) 985-3608

Kinfield

Big Race

The Heavyweight Ski Contest at the Sugarloaf Resort attracts 20,000 pounds of contestants each year. Some tip the scales at 400 pounds—so watch out below! No charge at all to be a spectator.
Time: 1st week in Apr.
Place: ME 16 and ME 27.
Contact: (207) 237-2000

Lubec

FDR's Summer Home

Visitors to the Roosevelt Campobello International Park can tour Franklin D. Roosevelt's 34-room "cottage" on Campobello Island. Free films are shown in the visitor center.
Time: Cottage tours: mid-May-mid-Oct., 9 a.m.-5 p.m.
Place: 1.5 mi. E off ME 189 on Campobello Island.
Contact: (207) 255-3475

Lynchville

Exotic Signpost

Touristy, yes, but true—a signpost pointing to Norway, Paris, Denmark, Naples, Sweden, Poland, Mexico, Peru and China—none of which (as towns in Maine) is more than 94 miles from the middle of Lynchville.
Place: Jct. ME 5 and ME 35.

Newry

Covered Bridge

Of the state's original 120, only ten covered bridges remain. Known as the "artist's bridge," the one over the Sunday River in Newry is the most photographed and painted bridge in the state. It's said that more paint has been used to portray it on canvas than to protect its wood from the weather!

Ogunquit

Maine's Monterey

Artists are attracted to this scenic section of Maine, now a thriving art community. At Perkins Cove, follow the Marginal Way, a walk which takes you along the sea for one mile—spectacular and reminiscent of California's Monterey Peninsula.

Orono

Come to Life

The University of Maine Anthropological Museum, certainly one of the best in the Northeast, brings varied cultures to life. Its displays range from local birchbark canoes to African masks and Eskimo dioramas.
Time: Mon.-Fri., 9 a.m.-3:30 p.m., or by appt.
Place: South Stevens Hall on University at Maine campus.
Contact: (207) 581-7102

Pembroke

Natural Spectacle

The reversing saltwater falls, a most unusual sight, is located near Pembroke on Leighton's Neck. Incoming tides rush between Mahar's Point and Falls Island at a 25-knot clip, reversing on the ebb tide. The water striking the rocky coastline causes a set of falls.
Time: Get tidal information from local residents.

Portland

Free Organ Concerts

The City of Portland sponsors a series of free organ concerts from mid-July to late August on Friday evenings at the Portland City Hall Auditorium. Don't miss the sounds of the world-famous Kotzschmar organ.
Time: Mid-July-late Aug., Fri., 8:15 p.m.
Place: Portland City Hall
Contact: (207) 775-5451

MAINE

Portland

Lighthouse

George Washington appointed the first lighthouse keeper for this famous landmark, built in 1790. It is the best-known lighthouse on the northeast coast and draws 60,000 visitors a year.

Time: 8 a.m.-4 p.m.
Place: Casco Bay.
Contact: (207) 799-2661
Note: Visitors are not allowed into the lighthouse itself.

Prohibition

Neal Dow, temperance crusader, Quaker and presidential candidate, drafted the world-famous "Maine Law" in the study of this federal-style mansion. His proposal became the 18th Amendment, which prohibited the sale of alcohol in this country until it was repealed. Free tours are now offered of this historic house.

Time: Tours: Mon.-Sat., 11 a.m.-4 p.m.
Place: 714 Congress St.
Contact: (207) 773-7773

Walking Tours

Four free brochures describe historic paths which you can take on walking tours of this interesting town. They are entitled "Guide to State Street," "Guide to Congress Street," "Historic Portland," "Guide to the Old Port Exchange." For free copies, write or call one of the contacts below.

Contact: Greater Portland Landmarks, Inc., 165 State St., Portland, ME 04101; (207) 774-5561. Or try the Greater Portland Chamber of Commerce, 142 Free St., Portland, ME 04101; (207) 772-2811.

Rockland

Andrew Wyeth

In the William A. Farnsworth Museum you'll find one of the country's finest collections of Andrew Wyeth's paintings, as well as other works by prominent 19th- and 20th-century American painters. Not to be missed.

Time: June-Sept., Mon.-Sat., 10 a.m.-5 p.m.; Sun., 1-5 p.m. Rest of year, same hours but closed Mon.
Place: 19 Elm St.
Contact: (207) 596-6457

Seafood Festival

In an average year, 35,000 people attend the Seafood Festival, which includes a lobster meal (not free), and free events such as live music (or comedy shows), pageants and crafts demonstrations.

Time: Late July-early Aug.
Place: Fishermen's Memorial Pier and Festival Grounds.
Contact: (207) 596-6631

Ship to Shore

The Shore Village Museum contains over 1,000 Coast Guard artifacts: lighthouse equipment, horns, bells and lifesaving gear. A treat for closet mariners.

Time: June-Sept., Mon.-Sat., 10 a.m.-5 p.m.; Sun., 1-5 p.m. Rest of year, Mon.-Fri., 10 a.m.-4 p.m.
Place: 104 Limerick St., in DAR Hall.
Contact: (207) 594-4950

Tuberous Begonias

More than 60 varieties of tuberous begonias bloom in the sunken garden surrounding a brook at Ureneff Tuberous Begonia Garden. A must if you're a fan of flowers and rich, velvety colors.

Time: July-late Sept., 8 a.m.-5 p.m.
Place: 169 Camden St., on US 1.
Contact: (207) 594-8095

Skowhegan

World's Largest Wooden Indian

A 62-foot statue, sculpted from pine, depicts a Native Ameri-

can fisherman dressed in buckskin and feathers. Great for posing snapshots!
Place: Pleasant St. and Madison Ave.
Contact: (207) 474-3621

Stonington

Miniature New England

Here's a miniature village, 16 buildings representing a typical New England hamlet. They were built by a local resident as a hobby, and so many people commented on them that he left them out in a garden for all to see.
Time: June-Sept., sunrise to sunset.
Place: ME 15 on E edge of town.
Contact: (207) 367-2351

Waterville

American Portraits

Colby College Museum of Art has a large collection of 19th-century American portraits. Two dozen are always on display. Also popular are the watercolors by Winslow Homer and the many changing exhibits.
Time: Mon.-Sat., 10 a.m.-4:30 p.m. (closed for lunch); Sun., 2-4:30 p.m.
Place: Colby College campus.
Contact: (207) 873-1131

Wells

Marsh Birds

The Rachel Carson National Wildlife Refuge, consisting of nine parcels of land and water, preserves a saltwater marsh which attracts 175 to 200 species of birds each year, including great blue herons and snowy egrets. Best birding is in May, June, September and October.
Time: Sunrise to sunset.
Place: 2.5 mi. N on ME 9E.
Contact: (207) 646-9226

West Paris

Maine Minerals

Cutting and polishing demonstrations add a special touch to Perham's Maine Mineral Store, noted for its extensive display of fine specimens collected in quarries throughout the state.
Time: Mon.-Sat., 9 a.m.-5 p.m.; Sun., 2-5 p.m.
Place: Jct. of ME 26 and ME 219.
Contact: (207) 674-2341

Winter Harbor

Lobster Boat Races

During the Lobster Boat Races, about the only thing you have to pay for is the lobster feed!

The races, dance on the wharf and spectacular fireworks display (one of the best in Maine) all come free.
Time: Early Aug.
Place: Wharf area.
Contact: (207) 963-2235

Statewide

Fall Color

To help you enjoy the colors and sights of Maine in the fall, the Conservation Department has prepared a free brochure listing 11 driving tours which include scenic routes, orchards, covered bridges and fall festivals. Ask for the Fall

MAINE

Statewide

Foliage brochure from the contact below.

Contact: Maine State Development Office, 193 State St., Augusta, ME 04333; (207) 289-2656.

Free Camping

Most information on camping leads you to areas where there's an access fee or overnight camping charge. But in fact, there are many areas owned by paper companies or managed by the state where you won't have to pay a dime. For information on these, write or call one of the contacts below.

Contact: Paper Industry Information Office, 133 State St., Augusta, ME 04330; (207) 622-3166. Or try the State of Maine, Bureau of Parks and Recreation, Dept. of Conservation, State House, Augusta, ME 04333; (207) 289-3821.

Free Fishing

Maine's coastal waters abound in mackerel, cod, haddock, halibut, flounder and sea bass. Fishing is free along the coastline, one of the most beautiful in the country.

Contact: Department of Inland Fisheries and Wildlife, 284 State St., Augusta, ME 04330; (207) 289-2571.

Gold Rush

With prices soaring, panning for gold is again popular. While Maine may not be well known as a panner's paradise, its streams do indeed produce pay dirt. Suggested streams include Black Mountain Brook, the East Branch of the Swift River, Gold Brook, Kibby Stream, the St. Croix River, Sandy River, and South Branch-Penobscot River.

Place: Ask locally for directions to prime sites.

Hiking

There's a fee charged to get into all state parks, but there are dozens of superb hikes in areas with free access, including state forests. Ask for the "Hiking in Maine" sheets from the contact below.

Contact: The Maine Publicity Bureau, 97 Winthrop St., Hallowell, ME 04347; (207) 289-2423.

Lighthouses

Dozens of photogenic lighthouses dot the coast and offshore islands, making this area one of the state's primary attractions for sightseers and photographers. One of the finest is Pemaquod Point Lighthouse, a 79-foot white tower on the west side of the entrance to Muscongus Bay.

Scenic Highways

The official state highway map outlines six outstanding scenic routes in bold green strokes. The map is free of charge from the contact below.

Contact: The Maine Publicity Bureau, 97 Winthrop St., Hallowell, ME 04347; (207) 289-2423.

Wild Blueberries

Pick all the wild blueberries you can find. They're plentiful in a state where this is an important cash crop (Washington County alone accounts for 90% of the nation's blueberries, to the tune of 15 million pounds).

Time: Berries ripen mid-July-Aug., depending upon location.

Place: Ask locally for spots.

MARYLAND

ATTRACTIONS·THE BEST FREE
THE ACTIONS·
FREE HE BEST
ATTRA ST FREE
THE BE ACTIONS·
FREE AT HE BEST
ATTRACTI ST FREE
THE BEST ACTIONS·
ATTRACTIO REE
THE BEST ONS·
FREE ATTRA BEST
ATTRACTIONS·THE BEST FREE
THE BEST FREE ATTRACTIONS·

Cumberland

Baltimore

ANNAPOLIS

MARYLAND

Aberdeen

Weaponry

The US Army Ordnance Museum has an extensive display of weapons from the Revolution to the present. Included are tanks, missiles, machine guns and mortars.

Time: Tues.-Fri., noon-5 p.m.; Sat.-Sun., 10 a.m.-5 p.m.
Place: Aberdeen Proving Ground.
Contact: (301) 278-3602

Annapolis

Free Concerts

During July and August, take in free concerts on the city dock on Tuesday evenings—at no charge whatsoever!

Time: July-Aug., Tues., 8 p.m.
Place: Annapolis City Dock.
Contact: (301) 269-3517

Naval Academy

There's no charge to tour the United States Naval Academy without a guide. Here you'll find the crypt and sarcophagus of John Paul Jones, often nicknamed the "father of the US Navy." Don't miss the noontime brigade formations, daily in front of Bancroft Hall.

Time: Visitor center: June-Sept., 9 a.m.-5 p.m.; rest of year, 10 a.m.-4 p.m.

Place: Visitor Gate, King George St.
Contact: (301) 267-3363

Ship Models

In the US Naval Academy Museum you'll find a wide

assortment of uniforms, flags, swords and ship models. The latter are incredibly detailed, so don't be surprised if the time flies by as you look at them.

Time: Mon.-Sat., 9 a.m.-5 p.m.; Sun., 11 a.m.-5 p.m.
Place: Preble Hall, US Naval Academy.
Contact: (301) 263-6933

State Capitol

The exact spot where Washington resigned his commission as commander-in-chief of the Continental Army is marked by a plaque in the Maryland State House—the oldest state capitol in the United States in continuous legislative use. At the visitor center you can see a slide presentation about the State House.

Time: Tours: 9 a.m.-4:30 p.m.
Place: State Cir.
Contact: (301) 269-3400

Dress Parades

Here's one of those moments you won't forget: a chance to watch a full-dress parade at the US Naval Academy. The spit-and-polish show is worth a detour.

Time: Wed., 3:45 p.m. (usually Apr. and Sept.).
Place: Worden Field, US Naval Academy.
Contact: (301) 267-3363

Baltimore

Clipper Ship

When *The Pride of Baltimore* comes to port each spring, there's no charge to see her. She's an exact replica of a Baltimore Clipper from the early

1800s. Get details of boarding times from the contact below.
Time: Late Apr.-mid-May, noon-6 p.m.
Place: Inner Harbor.
Contact: (301) 752-8632

Star-Spangled Banner

The Fort McHenry National Monument preserves the setting which inspired Francis Scott Key to write the "Star-Spangled Banner." Be sure to see the 15-minute film before walking the grounds.
Time: Mem. Day-Labor Day, 9 a.m.-8 p.m.; rest of year, 9 a.m.-5 p.m.
Place: End of Fort Ave.
Contact: (301) 962-4290

Impressionist Collection

The Baltimore Museum of Art is a treasure trove of impressionist paintings, colonial silver, furniture and sculpture. Well-represented are Cézanne, Matisse, Monet and Picasso.
Time: Tues.-Sat., 11 a.m.-5 p.m.; Sun., 1-5 p.m.
Place: Art Museum Dr., Wyman Park.
Contact: (301) 396-7100

Portrait Collection

The Maryland Historical Society displays 250 portraits of famous Marylanders, the original manuscript of the "Star-Spangled Banner," and a 19th-century double parlor.
Time: Tues.-Sat., 11 a.m.-4 p.m.; Sun., 1-5 p.m.
Place: 201 W. Monument St.
Contact: (301) 685-3750

Ethnic Festivals

Throughout the summer, 20 ethnic festivals are held in Baltimore's Inner Harbor. These run the gamut from Afghan to Ukrainian. The City Fair in September is the best-known and one of the most popular celebrations of them all. Get a free brochure from the contact below.
Contact: Baltimore Office of Promotion and Tourism, 110 W. Baltimore St., Baltimore, MD 21201; (301) 752-8632.

Lexington Market

In two brick buildings covering two city blocks, you'll find everything from wriggling eels to freshly-baked breads. The market dates back to 1782 and is the largest of its kind in the US. A feast of sights and smells!
Time: Mon.-Sat., 8:30 a.m-6 p.m.
Place: Entaw and Lexington Sts.
Contact: (301) 685-6169

Tea and Cookies

More than 30 million cups of tea are poured each year in the US McCormick Spice Company. A 28-minute movie and tour will fill you in on the lore of the world's favorite drink, popularized in Great Britain during the reign of Elizabeth I. Tea-tasting follows, of course.
Time: Tours: 10 a.m. and 1:30 p.m., by appt. only.
Place: Friendship Court, 414 Light St.
Contact: (301) 547-6166

Old Shot Tower

The Old Shot Tower, built in 1828 and used until 1892, is famous for the fine shot once made in it. Molten lead was dropped 234 feet through layers of screen into buckets of water below, where it cooled immediately into the quality product. A visit includes an audio-visual presentation.
Time: Wed.-Sun., 10 a.m.-4 p.m.
Place: E. Fayette and Front Sts.
Contact: (301) 539-8209

Peale Paintings

The oldest museum building in the US, the Peale Museum (1814) contains an extensive collection of prints, paintings and photographs related to Baltimore, as well as many paintings by members of the Peale family.
Time: Tues.-Fri., 10:30 a.m.-4:30 p.m.; Sat.-Sun., 1-5 p.m.
Place: 225 N. Holliday St.
Contact: (301) 396-3523

MARYLAND

Baltimore

Stunning Gardens

Imagine 100,000 tulips and other bulbs in bloom during the early spring, or the sight of 5,000 azaleas and other flowering shrubs in full color. This just begins to describe the peak season at Sherwood Gardens, usually running from late April to early May.
Time: Sunrise to sunset.
Place: Highfield Rd. and Greenway.
Contact: (301) 396-7900

Free Music

The building itself is impressive, and the music even more so, at the Peabody Conservatory of Music. You can attend many free recitals and concerts during the academic year. Write or call the conservatory for a brochure with scheduled performances.
Contact: Peabody Conservatory of Music, 1 E. Mount Vernon Place, Baltimore, MD 21202; (301) 837-0600.

Art Exhibits

The Walters Art Gallery has a large collection covering works of art from Egyptian times to early 20th-century pieces. The original gallery building, a Renaissance structure finished in 1906, is constructed of marble and other stone. An adjoining building was opened in 1974.
Time: Mon., 1 p.m.-5 p.m.; Tues.-Sat., 11 a.m.-5 p.m.; Sun., 2-5 p.m.
Place: N. Charles and Centre Sts.
Contact: (301) 547-9000

Beltsville

Experimental Farm

At the Agricultural Research Center you'll learn about experimentation going on in this field. There's a push-button exhibit telling you about the center and a two-hour tour. When you take the tour, you'll stop at the dairy parlor (where cows are milked) and at the conservatory, filled with plants undergoing tests.
Time: Mon.-Fri., 8 a.m.-4:30 p.m.
Place: Powder Mill Rd.
Contact: (301) 344-2483

Berlin

Isolated Beach

There's no charge to use Assateague State Park during weekdays. Here you'll find isolated stretches of dunes, ideal for swimming and photography.
Time: Free Mon.-Fri. only; charge on weekends.
Place: 5 mi. E on MD 376, then 5 mi. S on MD 611.
Contact: Assateague State Park, Rte. 2, P.O. Box 293, Berlin, MD 21811; (301) 641-2120.

Cambridge

Thick with Ducks

Black ducks, mallards, teal and Canada geese swarm into Blackwater National Wildlife Refuge which has an observation tower, five miles of road winding through wildlife areas and a visitor center with films. As many as 225 bird species have been seen here in one week. Best in late fall and winter.
Time: Refuge: sunrise to sunset. Center: June-Aug., Mon.-Fri., 7:30 a.m.-4 p.m. Rest of year, Mon.-Sat., 7:30 a.m.-4 p.m.; Sun., 9:30 a.m.-4 p.m.
Place: 11 mi. S of town via US 50 or MD 16/335.
Contact: (301) 228-2677

Cayots

Horse Farm

Visitors are welcome to Windfields Farm, home of famous race horses including Northern Dancer. Best time to visit is in late spring when barns are filled with 200 to 300 horses, including some only months old.
Time: Mon.-Fri., 9 a.m.-4 p.m.
Place: 3 mi. E of town on MD 310,

then S 2 mi. on St. Augustine Rd. (Bunker Hill Rd.).
Contact: (301) 755-6706

Charlotte Hall

Amish Auction

At the Farmers Market and Auction, join the crowd as Amish farmers auction off everything from antiques to ponies.
Time: Wed., Sat., 8 a.m.-5 p.m.
Place: Along MD 5.
Contact: (301) 884-3966

Chestertown

Colonial Architecture

For the pure beauty of its colonial-style homes, the town of Chestertown is worth visiting. Simply walk or drive along its streets to appreciate these lovely buildings. Bring your camera!

Emmitsburg

Catholic Shrine

Particularly of interest to Roman Catholics is the first National Catholic Shrine in the US, a Lourdes Grotto replica. On the grounds of St. Joseph's Provincial House is the Mother Elizabeth Ann Seton Shrine, which honors the first native-born American saint. There's also an orientation film that will provide you with background information.
Time: 10 a.m.-5 p.m.; please call in advance.
Place: S. Seton Ave.
Contact: (301) 447-6606

Frederick

Rose Hill Manor

Rose Hill Manor Children's Museum was once the 18th-century home of Maryland's first governor. Now children can "play" history here in "touch and feel" exhibits. In the carriage house you'll find 15 restored carriages and sleighs.
Time: Apr.-Oct., Mon.-Sat., 10 a.m.-4 p.m.; Sun., 1-4 p.m. (closed Jan.-Feb.).
Place: 1611 N. Market St.
Contact: (301) 694-1650 or 663-8687

Grantsville

Colonial Crafts

At Penn Alps you'll see artisans working on arts and crafts typical of the colonial era, from yarn spinning to pottery making.
Time: Feb.-Dec.; call for hours, which are variable.
Place: .5 mile E on US 40.
Contact: (301) 895-5985

Great Falls

Down the Old Potomac

Stop off at Great Falls Tavern to take in a film called "Down The Old Potomac." You'll then know about this area with its abandoned C & O Canal—picturesque and ideal for hikes.
Time: 9 a.m.-5 p.m.
Place: 11710 MacArthur Blvd.
Contact: (301) 299-2026

Greenbelt

Space Exploration

At the NASA/Goddard Visitor Center are exhibits on rockets,

MARYLAND

Greenbelt

satellites and space exploration. Bounce a phone conversation 44,000 miles off a satellite, talk to a computer named Victor, visit the planetarium and climb into a Gemini training capsule. Absolutely worth seeing.
Time: Wed.-Sat., 10 a.m.-4 p.m.
Place: Exit 22A off Baltimore Pkwy.
Contact: (301) 344-8981

Hagerstown
Oriental Art

Overlooking a lake, the Washington County Museum of Fine Arts features changing exhibits, Sunday afternoon concerts and a small permanent collection with fine Oriental pieces including jades.
Time: Tues.-Sat., 10 a.m.-5 p.m.; Sun., 1-6 p.m.
Place: On US 11 in City Park.
Contact: (301) 739-5727

Kensington
Award-Winning Landscape

At the Mormon Temple Visitor Center you're invited to tour the temple gardens and see any number of inspirational films on request. The grounds, 57 acres in all, have been recognized with numerous awards.
Time: 10 a.m.-9 p.m.
Place: 9900 Stoneybrook Dr.
Contact: (301) 587-0144

Lilypons
Goldfish Farm

At Three Springs Fisheries you're at the world's largest goldfish and waterlily farm. It boasts 1,800 acres of blooming ponds stocked with a wide variety of ornamental fish, from fringetail Calicos to the golden beauties you see at your local Woolworth's.
Time: Mon.-Sat., 9 a.m.-3 p.m.; Sun., 1-3 p.m. (lilies: best bloom late May-Aug.).
Place: Lilypons Rd.
Contact: (301) 874-5133

Matapeake
Chesapeake Bay in Miniature

The Chesapeake Bay Study and Hydraulic Model Complex has a scale model of the Chesapeake Bay area, reproducing the tides for study purposes. The 14-acre shelter houses the largest model of this kind in the world.
Time: Tours: Mon.-Fri., 10 a.m., 1 and 3 p.m.
Place: On Kent Island near town.
Contact: (301) 962-4616

Oakland
Swallow Falls

Edison, Firestone and Ford camped next to Swallow Falls in the state park of the same name in 1918. Muddy Creek Falls, in the same park, is more impressive yet, as it tumbles down 51 feet of rocks. Ideal for picnics and short hikes.
Place: 9 miles NW of town on Cty. Rd. 20.
Contact: (301) 334-9180
Note: There are two Oaklands in Maryland. This one is near Mountain Lake Park, in the far western end of the MD panhandle.

Oxon Hill
Living Farm

Oxon Hill Farm demonstrates turn-of-the-century farm machinery. Here you'll also find a variety of farm animals—a delight to children.
Time: 8 a.m.-5 p.m.
Place: Off I-95 and Oxon Hill Rd.
Contact: (301) 839-1177

Princess Anne

Delmarva Chicken Festival

Delmarva (Delaware, Maryland, Virginia) claims to be "the birthplace of America's broiler industry." In the birds' honor there are chicken scratching, rooster calling and even chicken plucking contests! But not for chickens! Be sure to consult the contact for the exact time and location.

Time: Early June.
Place: Call for location, which varies.
Contact: (302) 856-2971

St. Mary's City

Maryland Day Celebration

On a chilly March day, Maryland celebrates with a gathering that is symbolic of the first Maryland General Assembly in 1676. The event is held at an exact replica of the first State House.

Time: Mar. 29.
Place: Old State House.
Contact: (301) 994-0779

Sharpsburg

Bloodiest Battle

The visitor center at the Antietam National Battlefield site has a fine film telling about America's bloodiest one-day battle.

Time: Center: June-Labor Day, 8:30 a.m.-6:30 p.m.; rest of year, 8:30 a.m.-5 p.m.
Place: 1 mi. N on MD 65.
Contact: (301) 432-5124

Hiking Trails

The demise of the C & O Canal has meant something special to hikers, bikers and backpackers. They will find the two paths along the abandoned waterway ideal for recreation. Get full information from the contact listed below.

Contact: Superintendent, C & O Canal National Historic Park, P.O. Box 4, Sharpsburg, MD 21782.

Silesia

Torchlight Tours

In the pale light of a full moon, step across the drawbridge of Fort Washington into the year 1861. Tour the 19th-century fortification and talk to staff members dressed as soldiers by the light of torches in the

battlements. Civil War-vintage small arms and cannon are fired on Sundays.

Time: Fort: 8 a.m.-sunset. Torchlight tours: May-Oct., evenings of full moon (call for exact dates).
Place: Fort Washington Rd., off MD 210.
Contact: (301) 292-2112

Solomons Island

Chesapeake Bay Craft

The Calvert Marine Museum has a fine collection of Chesa-

MARYLAND

Solomons Island

peake Bay water craft, from clam and oyster dredge boats to a 34-foot log canoe.

Time: May-Sept., Sat., 10 a.m.-5 p.m.; Sun., 1-5 p.m. Rest of year, Tues.-Fri., 10 a.m.-4:30 p.m.; Sat.-Sun., 1-4:30 p.m.
Contact: (301) 326-3719

Suitland

Aircraft Restoration Shop

Silver Hill Museum is the place where aircraft for the Smithsonian's Air and Space Museum are restored before they're put on display. Tours last two hours and must be booked in advance, but they're worth the planning. Calls for reservations are to the Smithsonian museum in Washington.

Time: Wed. and Fri., 10 a.m.; Sat.-Sun., 10 a.m. and 1 p.m., by reservation made 2 weeks in advance.
Place: Old Silver Hill Rd.
Contact: (202) 357-1400

Thurmont

Blue Blazes Still

This is an operating still, but nowadays it's run by the feds. It's on the spot of a once-illegal still which did very well indeed during Prohibition.

Time: Mem. Day-Oct., Sat.-Sun., sunrise to sunset.
Place: Catoctin Mountain Park, 3 mi. W of town on MD 77.
Contact: (301) 824-2574

Towson

Georgian Mansion

The Hampton National Historic Site preserves an elegant Georgian mansion (1790). The home and gardens are undergoing constant restoration, and the site is certainly worth a stop.

Time: Tues.-Sat., 11 a.m.-5 p.m.; Sun., 1-5 p.m.
Place: 535 Hampton Ln.
Contact: (301) 823-7054

Power Tools

The Black and Decker Museum of Progress chronicles the development of tools—from drills made of walrus ribs to torqueless space wrenches.

Time: Tues.-Thurs., 1-4 p.m.
Place: 701 E. Joppa Rd.
Contact: (301) 828-3709

Statewide

Championship Jousts

Jousting is Maryland's state sport. Knights no longer knock each other off horses but try to spear suspended rings while galloping by at full speed—wonderful to watch. Of the 16 or so jousting tournaments, only a few charge a fee. For a schedule, contact the state's jousting association.

Contact: Maryland Jousting Tournament Assoc., 2516B Jefferson Pike, Jefferson, MD 21755; (301) 834-8371.

Free Fishing

Striped bass (locally known as rockfish), bluefish, weakfish and channel bass—these are free for the taking in saltwater areas, where no license is required. The same is true for recreational crabbing, one of the region's most delightful

pastimes. Write and ask specifically for the "Tidewater Fishing Guide" from the contact below.

Contact: Tidewater Administration, Dept. of Natural Resources, Tawes State Office Bldg., Annapolis, MD 21401; (301) 269-3765.

Free Day in the Parks

Take advantage of the free entry policy in Maryland's 35 state parks on Mondays. For information, contact the state's park service.

Contact: Maryland Park Service, Tawes State Office Bldg., Annapolis, MD 21401; (301) 269-3761.

MASSACHUSETTS

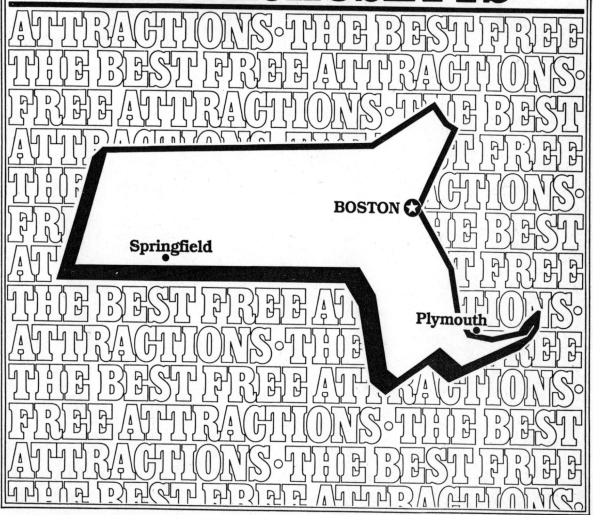

ATTRACTIONS·THE BEST FREE
THE BEST FREE ATTRACTIONS·
FREE ATTRACTIONS·THE BEST
ATTRACTIONS·THE BEST FREE
THE BEST FREE ATTRACTIONS·
FREE ATTRACTIONS·THE BEST
ATTRACTIONS·THE BEST FREE
THE BEST FREE ATTRACTIONS·
ATTRACTIONS·THE BEST FREE
THE BEST FREE ATTRACTIONS·
FREE ATTRACTIONS·THE BEST
ATTRACTIONS·THE BEST FREE
THE BEST FREE ATTRACTIONS·

BOSTON

Springfield

Plymouth

MASSACHUSETTS

Andover

Hand-Spun Textiles

At the Merrimack Textile Museum, watch raw wool being spun into tweeds and woolens. Skilled weavers demonstrate their craft on both hand-operated and power looms.

Time: Tues.-Sat., 10 a.m.-4 p.m.; Sun., 1-5 p.m.
Place: 800 Massachusetts Ave.
Contact: (617) 686-0191

American Art

A panorama of American art from the 18th through the 20th centuries—definitely one of Andover's best collections. Works at the Addison Gallery include American paintings, sculpture, drawings, prints and photographs—even ship models.

Time: Sept.-July, Tues.-Sat., 10 a.m.-5 p.m.; Sun., 2:30-5 p.m. Closed Aug. and holidays.
Contact: (617) 475-7515

Attleboro

Tropical Rain Forest

View the tropical flora and fauna blooming in Capron Park's rain forest. Or stroll through the rose and rock gardens. For animal lovers (and kids) there's a zoo, mon-

key house and aviary. Top off the visit with a picnic.

Time: May-Sept., 7:30 a.m.-9 p.m.; Oct.-Apr., 7:30 a.m.-4 p.m.
Place: 1 mi. W of town on MA 123.
Contact: (617) 222-3047

Barre

Pine Plantation

Forty acres of natural beauty—upland woodland, pine plantation, pond and brook. Take one of the many trails through this memorable setting. For more information on Cook's Canyon, write to the contact below.

Contact: P.O. Box 638, Barre, MA 01005; (617) 355-4064.

Boston

Bunker Hill

View firsthand the site and some of the relics of this legendary American battle. The Bunker Hill Museum offers a special slide and taped program. History buffs might enjoy seeing the Bunker Hill Monument, a 221-foot granite obelisk commemorating the battle. Be prepared to climb the spiral staircase to the top—no elevator.

Time: Bunker Hill Monument: 9 a.m.-dusk. Bunker Hill Museum: Apr.-Oct., Tues.-Sun., 10 a.m.-4 p.m.
Place: Monument: Monument Sq. Museum: 43 Monument Sq.
Contact: (617) 241-8220

Boston Marathon

Why read about it when you can see it? This famous 26-mile foot-race starts at Hopkinton and ends at the Prudential Center. (There's a fee to enter the marathon, but watching comes free.)

Time: 3rd Mon. in Apr.
Contact: (617) 426-1250

Downtown Walking Tour

Tour downtown Boston on foot—a well-marked trail will lead you past 16 points of historic interest. Other exhibits, monuments and shrines are just off the trail. For brochures, write or stop at the contact below.

Contact: Information Booth, Boston Common; the City Hall Hospitality Center and the National Park Visitor Center, 15 State St.

Free Concerts

Join a 50-year old tradition, and bring a blanket and a picnic dinner to a free concert of light classical and popular music by the Boston Pops. During every July, the orchestra presents concerts on the Esplanade, a public green in Boston.

Time: July 4 weekend plus about a week later in July. Schedule varies, but concerts usually begin at 8 p.m.
Place: Hatch Shell.
Contact: (617) 266-1492, 426-1250

George Washington's Personal Library

A book lover's dream—the Boston Athenaeum owns 430,000 books, including the personal library of George Washington. Also on display are priceless paintings and prints.

Time: Oct.-May, Mon.-Fri., 9 a.m.-5:30 p.m.; Sat., 9 a.m.-4 p.m.
Place: 10 1/2 Beacon St.
Contact: (617) 227-0270

State House

Be sure to view the unchanged facade on this beautiful old building, designed by Charles Bulfinch, one of America's first professional architects. Inside are various historical paintings and war relics. There's also an Archives Museum and a Hall of Flags. Visit the House and Senate Chambers on the third floor and watch the legislature in session.

Time: Mon.-Fri., 9 a.m.-5 p.m.; Sat.-Sun., 10 a.m.-3:30 p.m. Tours: Every 30 min., 10 a.m.-3:30 p.m. Closed Mar. 17, 3rd Mon. in Apr., June 17, other holidays except President's Day.
Place: Beacon St. at head of Park St.
Contact: (617) 223-0058, 727-2121

Exotic Cattle

The Franklin Park Zoo is sure to appeal to zoo visitors tired of the usual fare. A "Bird's World" aviary features an exhibit on African bird artifacts. Don't miss the hilltop range where you'll see camels, antelopes, deer, exotic cattle and sheep.

Time: May-Sept., 10 a.m.-4:30 p.m.; rest of year, 10 a.m.-4 p.m.
Place: End of Jamaicaway, Rte. 1 S.

Contact: (617) 442-2005, 442-0991

Museum of Fine Arts

Museum-goers shouldn't miss this one! Admission is charged most days, but there *is* a free-entry time. (Children under 16 are always admitted free.) Oriental, Indian, Mesopotanian, Egyptian, Greek, Roman, European, and American collections of art and textiles. Also early musical instruments. The museum provides excellent gallery talks, lectures, seminars, films and children's programs. Call about free concerts.

Time: Free Fri., 5-9 p.m.
Place: 465 Huntington Ave.
Contact: (617) 267-9300

Faneuil Hall and Quincy Market

Called the "Cradle of Liberty," Faneuil Hall (1742) served as a meeting hall during the revolutionary movement. Now, expanded and restored, it offers a number of noteworthy attractions. The popular Quincy, South and North Markets contain a variety of restaurants, boutiques—even produce stands! Upstairs is a military museum. Also worth visiting is the Museum of Fine Arts, which features changing art exhibits from the permanent

MASSACHUSETTS

Boston

collection of the Boston Museum of Fine Arts.

Time: Markets: Mon.-Fri., 9 a.m.-5 p.m.; Sat., 10 a.m.-5 p.m. Military Museum: Mon.-Fri., 10 a.m.-4 p.m.; closed 1st two weeks of Oct. Museum of Fine Arts: Tues.-Sat., 11 a.m.-7 p.m.; Sun., 1-5 p.m.
Place: Merchants Row.
Contact: (617) 523-8794

Globe of Glass

Walk across a glass bridge and into a giant globe of glass! This Mapparium is the special feature of a guided tour through the Christian Science Monitor's newspaper publishing facilities.

Time: May 1-Oct. 30, Mon.-Fri., 8 a.m.-4 p.m.; Sat., 9 a.m.-4 p.m.; Sun., noon-4:45 p.m. Rest of year, Sat. 10 a.m.-3:45 p.m.; Sun., noon-3:45 p.m. Tours: Mon.-Fri., 9:30 a.m., 11 a.m., 1:30 p.m. and 3 p.m.
Place: 1 Norway St.

"The British Are Coming!"

History was made here, when Paul Revere's lanterns hung from the steeple's highest window and signalled the departure of British troops. The original window is still there. See also the restored organ,

built in 1759, one of the earliest in North America.

Time: 9 a.m.-5 p.m.; Sun. services, 9:30 and 11 a.m., 4 p.m.
Place: 193 Salem St., at foot of Hull St.
Contact: (617) 523-6676

Old Ironsides

View firsthand this legendary, 44-gun frigate, built and launched in 1797, in the Boston Naval Historical Park. Paul Revere himself made the bolts and copper sheathing.

Time: 9:30 a.m.-3:50 p.m.
Place: Chelsea and Water St.
Contact: (617) 241-9078

Brewster

Drummer-Boy Museum

You'll see 21 life-sized paintings depicting scenes from the American Revolution. Observe the three-dimensional effects!

Time: May 15-Oct. 12, 9:30 a.m.-6 p.m. Tours last 50 minutes.
Place: 2 mi. W on MA 6A.
Contact: (617) 896-3823

Cambridge

Tree-Lover's Paradise

The Arnold Arboretum, the world's largest, contains over 6,000 varieties of trees and shrubs—all labeled. Follow the

lovely, winding walks past brilliant flower beds. Take special note of seasonal displays, with fragrant lilacs in spring and brilliant autumn colors. Also visit the library, herbarium, greenhouses and exhibition gallery.

Time: Buildings: June 20-Sept. 20, Mon.-Fri., 8:30 a.m.-4:30 p.m.; rest of year, 9 a.m.-5 p.m. Library, herbarium, exhibition gallery: sunrise to sunset.
Place: Arborway, Jamaica Plain.
Contact: (617) 524-1718

Art Treasurers

View the evolution of art from prehistoric to modern times at the Fogg Art Museum. Collections include ancient, Oriental and Greek art and a noted display of European art of the late 18th and early 19th centuries.

Time: Mon.-Fri., 9 a.m.-5 p.m.; Sat., 10 a.m.-5 p.m.; Sun., 2-5 p.m.
Place: 32 Quincy St. at Broadway.
Contact: (617) 495-2387

Walking Tours of Harvard

Sample the Harvard life by walking through the world-famous campus. When you're done, you can truthfully say you've gone to Harvard!

Time: Sept. 1-June 14, 11:15 a.m., 1:15 p.m., 2:15 p.m.; June 15-Aug. 31, Mon.-Sat.,

10 a.m., 11:15 a.m., 2:15 p.m., 3:15 p.m.; Sun., 1:30 p.m., 3 p.m. Tours last 45 min.
Place: School year: Byerly Hall, 8 Garden St. Summer: Holyoke Center Arcade, 1350 Massachusetts Ave.
Contact: (617) 495-1573

Ship Models

Boat lovers: steer straight to this one. The Hart Nautical Museum traces the development of ship and marine engineering. On display are rigged merchant and naval ship models and engine models—dating from 1,000 A.D. to the present.
Time: 9 a.m.-5 p.m. on weekends and holidays.
Place: 55 Massachusetts Ave., M.I.T. campus. Enter at 77 Massachusetts Ave.
Contact: (617) 253-5942

Cape Cod

Biker's Delight

Excellent bike paths plus magnificent landscape make Cape Cod an ideal place for biking. Wheel along the Cape Cod canal, through Cedar Banks and sand dunes, along Salt Meadow and by varied forests, ponds and bogs. Major trails located in Brewster, Cape Cod Canal, Cape Cod National Seashore and Falmouth.
Contact: Cathy Buckley, Central

Transportation Planning Staff, 27 School Street, Boston, MA 02108; (617) 523-3410. National Seashores: (617) 349-3785. Visitor centers available at Eastham and Provincetown.

Chatham

Morris Island Refuge

In addition to 252 species of birds, enjoy free surf fishing and beautiful views of Pleasant Bay, Monomoy Island and the Atlantic Ocean.
Place: Boat from Chatham, then take Main St. past Chatham Lighthouse, continue to Morris Island Rd. Hq. on Morris Island.
Contact: (617) 945-0594
Note: Pets allowed on leash only.

Concord

Minutemen's Last Stand

At the North Bridge Unit of the Minute Man National Historical Park, visit the reconstructed North Bridge over the Concord River and the famed minuteman statue by Daniel Chester French. The visitor center there offers exhibits and information. In the Battle Road Unit, you can travel an historic four-mile path and see

a movie shown at the visitor center.
Time: North Bridge Visitor Center: 8:30 a.m.-5 p.m. Battle Road Visitor Center: 8:30 a.m.-5 p.m.
Place: Minute Man National Historical Park: off MA 2A between Concord and Lexington. North Bridge Visitor Center: on Liberty St. Battle Road Visitor Center: off MA 2A in Lexington.
Contact: P.O. Box 160, Concord, MA 01742; (617) 369-6944.

Sleepy Hollow Cemetery

Buried here are some of the notables in American literature—Thoreau, Emerson,

MASSACHUSETTS

Concord

Hawthorne and the Alcotts. Watch out for Washington Irving's headless horseman who is said to gallop by on Halloween night.
Place: Bedfort St.
Contact: (617) 369-3120

Walden Pond

Walk through Thoreau's woods and visit the site of his cabin. Little remains here—just the solitude you can still enjoy. There are hiking trails and horseback-riding trails, but you must find your own horse.
Time: May-Sept., 10 a.m.-7 p.m.
Place: Walden Pond State Reservation, 915 Walden St., S of town.
Contact: (617) 369-3254

Antiquarian Museum

A visit here will round out your exposure to Concord's historic past. You'll view a diorama of the battle of Concord and Paul Revere's North Church lantern. Seventeen rooms full of artifacts will give you a glimpse of life in a New England town from the 17th to 19th centuries.
Time: Mar. 11-Oct. 31, Mon.-Sat., 10 a.m.-4:30 p.m.; Sun. 2-4:30 p.m.
Place: Lexington Rd. and Cambridge Turnpike.
Contact: (617) 369-9609

Great Meadows National Wildlife Refuge

These 3,000 acres of marsh, open water and upland offer something in every season. Bird lovers will appreciate the 216 species of birds. Plenty of trails and bike paths, an observation tower, photo blinds and an exhibit area. Winter activities include cross-country skiing and snowshoeing.
Time: Dawn to dusk.
Place: 2 mi. NE of town off MA 62.
Contact: 191 Sudbury Rd.; (617) 443-4661.
Note: No rentals are available; pets must be on leash.

Dalton

History of Papermaking

Tour this old stone mill, built in 1844, and learn about the history of American papermaking from the Revolution to the present. You'll see a scale model of a papermaking machine and examples of paper used for US currency at the Crane Museum.
Time: June-Sept., Mon.-Fri., 2-5 p.m.; Tues.-Thurs., 1-5 p.m.
Place: South St., 5 mi. E of town, off MA 9.
Contact: (413) 684-2600

Danvers

Old-Fashioned Candy Making

If you'd like to see how candy is made, visit Putnam Pantry. You'll also get a sample. The plant makes over 300 varieties of candies and ice cream. Hand-dipped chocolates are a specialty.
Time: Mon.-Fri., 9 a.m.-4:30 p.m.
Place: Downtown on US 1.
Contact: (617) 774-2383

Eastham

Cape Cod National Seashore

Ocean beaches, sand dunes, marshes, swamps, grasslands and wildlife—29,000 acres of Cape Cod's prime resources. Guided walking tours and evening lectures are offered in the summer. Trails for everyone: self-guided nature trails, bicycle trails, swamp trails and much more. Don't miss the high bluffs and look for azaleas by the fresh water. You can also go picnicking, swimming and surf fishing. Visitor centers in Eastham and Provincetown offer exhibits and interpretive programs.
Time: Salt Pond Visitor center in Eastham: late June-Labor

Day, 8 a.m.-6 p.m.; rest of year, 9 a.m.-5 p.m. Province Lands Visitor center: late June-Labor Day, 9 a.m.-6 p.m.; May 2-mid-June and day after Labor Day-mid-Nov., 9 a.m.-5 p.m.

Place: Cape Cod National Seashore: E off US 6. Province Lands Visitor center: Race Point Rd., near Provincetown. Headquarters: South Wellfleet.

Contact: Superintendent, Cape Cod National Seashore, S. Wellfleet, MA 02663; (617) 349-3785.

Note: Parking at beaches is free after Labor Day.

Easthampton

Arcadia Wildlife Sanctuary

You can explore 560 acres of woodland, meadow and marsh along the scenic Connecticut River. Get the best view of the marsh from the observation tower. Regular public programming, guided tours, two self-guiding trails (for children and adults) and a nature center.

Contact: (413) 584-3009

Fairhaven

Militia Color Ceremony

This preserved Revolutionary War fort saw its first naval battle on May 17, 1795. Witness a reenactment of the 4th Old Dartmouth Militia formal color ceremony at Fort Phoenix.

Time: June-Aug., Sun. nights.
Place: Green St.
Contact: (617) 999-5231

Gloucester

Seafood in the Making

Don't just visit Gloucester to eat its seafood, watch how it's prepared! At Gorton's you're invited to view the complete processing of frozen seafood from a special visitor's observation platform.

Time: Mon.-Fri., 9-11 a.m., noon-2 p.m., 2:30-4 p.m.
Place: 327 Main St.
Contact: (617) 283-3000

Hadley

Colonial Farm Household

At this restored 1782 barn, you learn what the typical farm household was like from Colonial times to the Civil War. Household and farm tools, a 15-seat stagecoach, an oxcart, a peddler's wagon, and early broom-making machinery. There's even a smithy to see.

Time: May 1-Oct. 12, Tues.-Sat., 10 a.m.-4:30 p.m.; Sun., 1:30-4:30 p.m.

Place: 147 Russell St., MA 9.
Contact: (413) 586-3920
Note: Children must be accompanied by an adult.

Hingham

Oldest Church in 13 Colonies

The Old Ship Church, built in 1681, is reputed to be the oldest church in the original 13 colonies. It has also been called the only 17th-century church in New England. The curved struts in its roof resemble the inverted hull of a ship!

Time: July-Aug., Tues.-Sun., noon-5 p.m.; other times by appt.
Place: Main St.
Contact: (617) 749-1679

New Bedford

Whaleman's Chapel

This chapel was described by Melville in *Moby Dick.* Take special note of the pulpit—it's shaped like the prow of a ship! Whalers' hazards are recorded on marble tablets.

Time: April-May, Sat., 10 a.m.-5 p.m.; Sun. 1-5 p.m. June-Aug., Mon.-Fri., 10 a.m.-5 p.m.; Sun., 1-5 p.m.
Place: Seaman's Bethel, 15 Johnny Cake Hill.
Contact: (617) 992-3295

MASSACHUSETTS

Newburyport

Clamming and Plum Picking

On Plum Island, the Parker River National Wildlife Refuge boasts miles of beach and sand dunes and many species of animals and plants. Migratory birds feed in the marshes. Activities include hiking, surf fishing, birdwatching, biking and plum picking.

Time: Year-round, dawn to dusk.
Place: Northern Blvd., 4 mi. SE on Plum Island.
Contact: (617) 465-5753

Northfield

300-Acre Reservoir and Pumping Plant

Tours of this 300-acre reservoir and underground hydroelectric plant take 50 minutes. The visitor center offers an informative film.

Time: Wed.-Sun., 9 a.m.-5:30 p.m.
Place: 7 mi. S of town on MA 63.
Contact: (413) 659-3714

Northhampton

Impressive Impressionists

Smith College has a noted collection of French impressionist paintings—Picasso, Degas, Corot, Courbet, Seurat. Be sure to call for an appointment.

Time: Sept. 15-May 31, Tues.-Sat., 11 a.m.-4:30 p.m.; Sun., 2:30-4:30 p.m. June, by appt. only.
Place: Elm St.
Contact: (413) 584-2700

North Truro

Historic Lighthouse

Even though it dates back to 1795, the Highland Light is still operated by the US Coast Guard, shining its powerful warning beam 20 miles out to vessels at sea. Tours of the dunes that surround it are available.

Time: Lighthouse tours: June-Aug.; times vary.
Place: In town.
Contact: (617) 487-1256

Orange

Scenic Drive— Mohawk Trail

Take this scenic drive between Orange and Williamstown— one of the state's best. Head west from Orange on MA 2 through Shelburne Falls, then along the Mohawk Trail to Williamstown.
Contact: (413) 339-4962

Parachute Jumping

More than 7,000 parachute jumps a year take place in

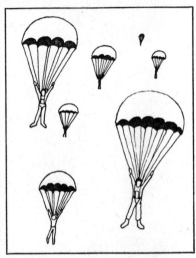

Orange. Watch the sky bloom with chutes as jumpers leap from planes above your head.
Time: Schedule depends on weather.
Contact: (617) 544-6911

Pittsfield

More than "Mush"

Peary's sledge is only one of the exhibits at the Berkshire Museum. You can also see mounted wildlife, life-like dioramas, geological exhibits, and works by old masters and Hudson River school artists.

Ask about movies and children's films.

Time: July-Aug., Mon.-Sat., 10 a.m.-5 p.m.; Sun., 2-5 p.m.; rest of year, same except closed Mon.
Place: 39 South St., on US 7.
Contact: (413) 442-6373

Melville Memorabilia

The public library in Pittsfield is noted for its fine collection of Herman Melville memorabilia—books, furniture, portraits and personal effects of the author. Get in touch with *Moby Dick*'s creator!

Time: Sept. 15-June 15, Mon.-Fri., 9 a.m.-9 p.m.; Sat., 9 a.m.-6 p.m. Rest of year, Mon., Wed., and Fri., 9 a.m.-9 p.m.; Tues., Thurs., and Sat., 9 a.m.-6 p.m.
Place: 1 Wendall Ave.
Contact: (413) 442-1559

Plymouth

Next Stop: New World

A legendary rock—the Pilgrims' first landing place in America. Sharing the site is a full-scale replica of the trusty *Mayflower*.

Place: Water St. on the harbor.
Contact: (617) 747-0961

Jenney Grist Mill Village

Pilgrims milled corn, wheat and rye 300 years ago in this water-powered grist mill, built in 1636. An explanation of the milling process and history of the site are provided. Look in at the craft and gift shops and smell the fresh-baked bread.

Time: May 1-Nov. 30, Tues.-Sun., 10 a.m.-5 p.m.; rest of year, daily, 10 a.m.-5 p.m.
Place: 8 Spring Ln. on Town Brook.
Contact: (617) 746-4604

Cranberry World

Cranberries are the pride of this museum, which depicts not only the berry's history, but its growing and harvesting process, its cooking uses—even cranberry art. You can visit actual working cranberry bogs and see cooking demonstrations. Free refreshments, guided tours and slide presentations!

Time: Apr. 1-Nov. 30, 10 a.m.-5 p.m.; closed Mon., Apr.-May, Oct.-Nov.
Place: Water St.
Contact: (617) 747-1000

Princeton

Hey-Day

Wachusett Meadow Wildlife Sanctuary—with 907 acres of meadow, ponds and brooks—draws thousands of visitors each fall to its annual Hey-Day. In addition to the wonderful trails, many come to view Crocker Maple, the fourth largest sugar maple in the US.

Contact: P.O. Box 268, Princeton, MA 01541; (617) 464-2712.

Rowley

Jewel Mill

With the power of its waterwheel, this mill grinds gems and rocks. Later, they're polished and assembled into jewelry. The mill, built in 1640, is one of the oldest in the 13 colonies. Guided tours explain the jewelry-making process. Another special attraction on the site is the oldest keystone bridge in the US.

Time: 9:30 a.m.-5:30 p.m.
Place: US 1 and Central St.
Contact: (617) 948-3974
Note: Children must be accompanied by an adult.

Salem

Needles and Pins

Salem's infamous witchcraft trials took place in this courthouse. You can examine trial

MASSACHUSETTS

Salem

documents and pins reportedly used by the witches to torment their victims.
Time: Mon.-Fri., 8 a.m.-4:30 p.m.
Place: Washington and Federal Sts.
Contact: (617) 774-1167 or 741-0200

Maritime National Historic Site

Shipbuilding, privateering and trading all occurred in the wharfs and buildings on Salem's historic waterfront. Of special interest is the Custom House, made famous by Nathaniel Hawthorne in *The Scarlet Letter*. Slide shows given here in the visitor center.
Time: Custom House: July-Labor Day, 8:30 a.m.-7 p.m.; rest of year, 8:30 a.m.-5 p.m. Ask for schedules of other buildings here.
Place: Custom House, 178 Derby St.
Contact: (617) 744-4323

Saugus

The Village Smithy

This historic site features an original 17th-century Iron-master's house, a museum and a reconstructed iron works—complete with blast furnace, forge, rolling and slitting mill. Guided tours and blacksmith demonstrations are offered.
Time: Apr. 1-Oct. 31, 9 a.m.-5 p.m.; rest of year, 9 a.m.-4 p.m.
Place: 244 Central St.
Contact: (617) 233-0500

Shelburne Falls

Bridge of Flowers

Brilliant flower beds border this 400-foot bridge across the Deerfield River. Special summer attractions include an outdoor art gallery on the Shelburne end of the bridge—and lighted flowers after dusk.
Place: On MA 2 along Mohawk Tr.
Contact: (413) 339-4962

South Hadley

Mysterious Rock Formations

This noted state park on top of Mt. Holyoke includes Titan's Piazza, a volcanic formation of overhanging rock columns, and Devil's Football, a 300-ton magnetic boulder. A superb view of the Connecticut Valley.
Time: Dawn-dusk.
Place: Joseph Allen Skinner State Park, 3 mi. N of town on MA 47.
Contact: (413) 538-2085

South Lincoln

Sheep-Shearing

Youngsters especially will enjoy the farm's domestic and wild animals. Other attractions include self-guiding nature trails in the wildlife sanctuary and spring sheep-shearing demonstrations. Special programs offered on weekends—all at Drumlin Farm.
Time: Sunrise-sunset.
Place: South Great Rd.
Contact: (617) 259-9807

Springfield

Polar Bears

This 800-acre park abounds in free entertainment. Musical

MASSACHUSETTS

shows at Barney Amphitheater, elephants and polar bears, a children's barnyard zoo (petting allowed), Trailside Museum, self-guiding nature trails and picnic facilities.
Time: 11 a.m.-4:30 p.m.
Place: Forest Park.
Contact: (413) 787-6440

30-Mile View

Next to Symphony Hall and the Civic Center is a 300-foot bell tower, similar to the one in the Piazza San Marco of Venice. You can climb to the top and be rewarded by a superb view of the Connecticut River Valley.
Time: Apr.-Oct., Mon.-Fri., 2:30-3:45 p.m.
Place: NW side of Court Sq.
Contact: (413) 736-2711
Note: An elevator in the bell tower will serve the less athletic.

French Tapestries

Here you can draw on the varied exhibits of several fine museums. Noted collections of ancient Chinese jades and porcelains, rugs and armored knights can be seen in the George Walter Vincent Smith Art Museum. The Museum of Fine Arts features Oriental, European and American art

(don't miss the French tapestries).
Time: George Walter Vincent Smith Museum: Tues.-Sat., 1-5 p.m.; Sun., 2-5 p.m. Museum of Fine Arts: Tues.-Sat., 1-5 p.m.; Sun., 2-5 p.m.
Place: George Walter Vincent Smith Museum: 222 State St. Museum of Fine Arts: 49 Chestnut St.
Contact: (413) 737-1750

Science Museum

Free Saturday movies and striking planetarium shows. There are also galleries full of mounted birds, animals and reptiles—plus a colorful aquarium and observatory.
Time: Tues.-Sat., 1-5 p.m.; Sun., 2-5 p.m.
Place: 236 State St.
Contact: (413) 732-4317

Organ of Rifles

This national historic site is noted for its museum featuring one of the world's most complete collections of small arms—from the first US musket (1795) to present-day weapons. Of special interest is the "Organ of Rifles," made famous by Henry Wadsworth Longfellow in his poem, "The Arsenal at Springfield."
Time: 8 a.m.-4:30 p.m.
Place: Federal St.

Contact: (413) 734-8551
Note: Children under 18 must be accompanied by a parent.

Stockbridge

Berkshire Garden Center

A gardener's delight—lovely gardens, a lily pond, rare trees, shrubs, wildflowers and herbs. Don't miss the special youth exhibits and demonstrations. Lectures and workshops also offered. Ask contact for details on the special flower show in August and the Harvest Festival in October.
Time: Apr.-Nov., 9 a.m.-5 p.m.
Place: 2 mi. W of town at jct. MA 102 and 183.
Contact: (413) 298-5530

Stoneham

Moated Animals

In the Walter D. Stone Memorial Zoo, animals are exhibited in outdoor enclosures—moats help keep them confined. You'll find nice picnic spots on the grounds.
Time: First Sun. in May-last Sat. in Oct., 10 a.m.-5 p.m.; rest of year, 10 a.m.-4:30 p.m.
Place: 149 Pond St.
Contact: (617) 438-3662

MASSACHUSETTS

Sudbury

Water-Powered Grist Mill

At Longfellow's Wayside Inn you can see water run down a sluiceway and power a 12-foot water wheel that drives a big grinding stone at a restored grist mill. The mill will give you a sense of the great potential for water power—in history and in the future. A donation is requested.

Time: Apr.-Oct., 9 a.m.-5 p.m.
Place: Wayside Inn Rd. (Old Boston Post Rd.)
Contact: (617) 443-8846

Sutton

Purgatory Chasm

The main attraction on this state reservation is Purgatory Chasm, a fissure about one-half mile long and 40 feet wide. Bring a picnic and enjoy the view.

Time: Daily to dark.
Place: .75 mi. N from MA 146, 4 mi. SE of town.
Contact: (617) 234-3733

Wales

Rare Wildflowers

Walk along the self-guiding trail at Norcross Wildlife Sanctuary, or take a motor tour through these 3,000 acres full of rare wildflowers. There are lots of native species of plants and animals, as well as two museums.

Time: Sanctuary: Mon.-Sat., 9 a.m.-4 p.m. Motor tours: 10 a.m., 1 p.m.
Place: W off MA 19 on Monson-Wales Rd.
Contact: R.D. #2, Monson, MA 01057; (413) 267-9654.
Note: Reservations required for motor tours. No private cars allowed in sanctuary.

Wareham

For Want of a Nail

Did you know you can date many antiques by examining the types of nails used in their construction? Visit this old mill building (1848) where an eight-minute movie vividly explains the history and process of nailmaking.

Time: June 1-Sept. 30, 1-4 p.m.
Place: 8 Elm St.
Contact: (617) 295-0038

Webster

Loooong Lake

The lake itself may not be terribly lengthy, but wait until you see its monicker: Lake Chargoggagoggmanchaug-gauggagoggchaubunagunga-

mau. Its meaning, translated from the Indian, makes good sense: "You fish on your side, I'll fish on my side, and nobody fishes in the middle."

Place: Next to MA 52 just S of MA 16.

As the World Turns

The Coleman Map Building can claim two of the world's largest items: the largest revolving globe (25 tons, 28 feet in diameter) and the largest relief map of the US (65 by 45 feet). Like the earth, the globe rotates daily and turns on its axis once a year. The relief model took 17 years to build.

Time: 10 a.m.-5 p.m.; other hours by appt.

Place: Babson College Campus, Babson Park, Forest St. and Wellesley Ave.
Contact: (617) 235-1200

Weston

World-Famous Stamp Collection

Stamp collectors flock to the Cardinal Spellman Philatelic Museum, a noted research center for the study of postage stamps. Cardinal Spellman's famous stamp collection includes over 300,000 stamps. Visit the library and museum store.
Time: Tues.-Thurs., 9:30 a.m.-3 p.m.; Sun., 2-5 p.m.; closed 1st 2 weeks in Aug.
Place: 235 Wellesley St.
Contact: (617) 894-6753

West Tisbury

Chicama Vineyards

A well-known vineyard in the southern part of Martha's Vineyard and the first bonded winery in Massachusetts, it offers tours of the vineyards, explanations of the winemaking process and, of course, wine tasting.
Time: June-Sept., Mon.-Sat., 1-5 p.m.; closed Sun.
Place: S on Cty. Rd. toward West Tisbury, then follow the Chicama Vineyards sign .2 mi.

after the West Tisbury sign.
Contact: (617) 693-0309

Wilbraham

Friendly Ice Cream

Tours guide you through the Friendly Ice Cream plant to see how ice cream is made and packaged. Over nine *million* gallons of ice cream (enough for 225 million cones) were produced in one recent year. A slide presentation describes history of the company, and you get a free ice cream souvenir.
Time: Mon.-Fri., 9, 10 and 11 a.m., by appt.
Place: 1855 Boston Rd. (Rte. 20).
Contact: (413) 543-2400
Note: Visitors must be at least 8 yrs. old and no cameras are allowed.

Williamstown

French Impressionists

In this beautiful estate is the Sterling and Francine Clark Art Institute, a noted collection of French impressionist paintings (works by Manet, Degas, Monet and Renoir) and rare old silver and porcelain. Sculpture by Rodin, Degas and Carpeaux.
Time: Tues.-Sun., 10 a.m.-5 p.m.
Place: Sterling and Francine

Clark Art Institute, South St., .5 mi. S of town.
Contact: (413) 458-8109

Williams College Museum of Art

This fine museum features European art, American paintings and African sculpture.
Time: Sept.-May, Mon.-Fri., 9 a.m.-5 p.m.; Sat.-Sun., 1-5 p.m.; rest of year, 1-5 p.m.
Place: Lawrence Hall, Williams College campus.
Contact: (413) 597-2429

Woods Hole

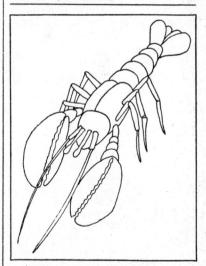

Marine Aquarium

Exhibits of live fish and marine life. Vivid displays

MASSACHUSETTS

Woods Hole

depict fish and lobster behavior and show how fish are tracked by sonar. Don't miss the seal pool!
Time: June 9-Sept. 9, 10 a.m.-4:30 p.m.; rest of year, by appt.
Place: Albatross St.
Contact: (617) 548-7684

Worcester

First Diner in America

While the food in this antique diner will cost you money, the view from the outside won't. Miss Worcester's shiny blue enamel with yellow trim will bring to mind late night roadstops and hundreds of old-time movie settings. A piece of Americana.
Time: Mon.-Fri., 5 a.m.-2 a.m.; Sat., 5 a.m.-2 p.m.
Place: 300 Southbridge.
Contact: (617) 752-4348

Statewide

Salt-Water Fishing

Much of Massachusetts's coast is suited to salt-water fishing from shore and can be especially good for two popular species, striped bass and blue fish. Four of the best places are the outer shores of Cape Cod, Plum Island, Sandy Neck Beach and Cape Cod Canal. The best time is from April through October. No license is needed.
Contact: Massachusetts Division of Marine Fisheries, Saltonstall State Office Bldg., 100 Cambridge St., Boston, MA 02202; (617) 727-3193.

NEW HAMPSHIRE

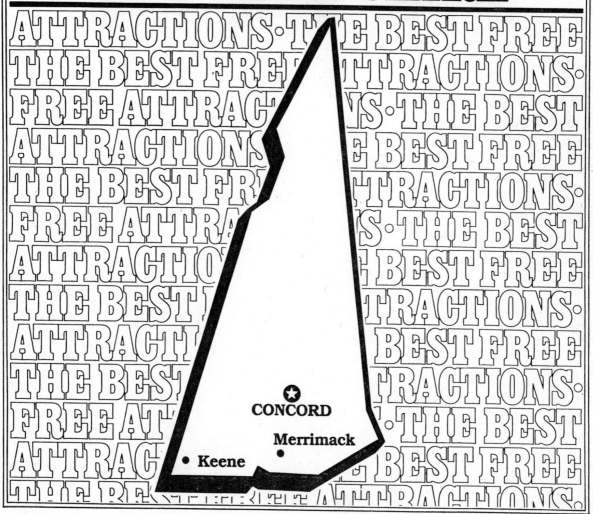

ATTRACTIONS·THE BEST FREE THE BEST FREE ATTRACTIONS· FREE ATTRACTIONS·THE BEST ATTRACTIONS·THE BEST FREE THE BEST FREE ATTRACTIONS· FREE ATTRACTIONS·THE BEST ATTRACTIONS·THE BEST FREE THE BEST FREE ATTRACTIONS· ATTRACTIONS·THE BEST FREE THE BEST FREE ATTRACTIONS· FREE ATTRACTIONS·THE BEST ATTRACTIONS·THE BEST FREE THE BEST FREE ATTRACTIONS·

★ CONCORD

Merrimack

● Keene

NEW HAMPSHIRE

Concord

Concord Coach

Here's the history of New Hampshire in period rooms, authentic period pieces, valuable silver and even a Concord coach—all found at the New Hampshire Historical Society.

Time: Mon.-Fri., 9 a.m.-4:30 p.m.
Place: 30 Park St.
Contact: (603) 225-3381

Hall of Flags

Three copies of amendments to the Constitution were discovered in a vault and have been preserved for all to see at the State House, the oldest in the country. Of particular interest is the colorful Hall of Flags.

Time: Sept.-May, Mon.-Fri., 8:30 a.m.-5 p.m. June-Sept., Mon. Fri., 8 a.m.-4:30 p.m.; Sat.-Sun., 9 a.m.-5 p.m.
Place: 107 N. Main St.
Contact: (603) 271-1110

Conway

Mountain Highway

One of the most popular and picturesque passages through the White Mountains is the Kancamagus Highway. Traveling west from Conway to Lincoln on NH 112, you encounter spectacular views of the surrounding mountains, forests and streams. Off the road are nice picnic spots.

Time: Late May-early Oct. Daytime traffic only, Dec.-mid-April.
Note: No stores or gas stations along the 34-mile route.

Crawford Notch

Scenic Stretch

Enjoy the majestic view along US 302 as it winds through Crawford Notch. Travel through the valley between wooded mountains until you reach the Silver Cascades, which fall near the highway. Worth the mile and a half inland trek are the stunning, 200-foot Arethusa Falls.

Place: US 302, between Twin Mountain and Glen.

Dover

17th-Century Home

In this historic 17th-century home, now the Woodman Institute, are natural history and science exhibits from Indian artifacts to mounted birds. Worth a short stop if you're in the area.

Time: Tues.-Sun., 2-5 p.m.; closed Feb.-mid-Mar.
Place: 182-192 Central Ave., .5 mi. S of town on NH 16.
Contact: (603) 742-1038

Enfield

Shaker Village

Stark granite buildings recreate the history of this former Shaker village. The visitor center features unique Shaker artifacts and period photographs. Also interesting is the La Salette Shrine, a replica of the beautiful shrine in France.

Time: June 15-Labor Day.
Place: US 4 to NH 4A, 5 mi. E of I-89.

Fitzwilliam

16-Acre Bed

The Rhododendron State Park is aptly named for the beautiful 16-acre bed of wild rhododendrons that bloom about mid-July. It's possibly the largest in the country. The park offers many foot trails with scenic views of the nearby mountains.

Time: Dawn to dusk. Blooming period in mid-July.
Place: 2.5 mi. SW of town, off NH 119.

Franconia

Spectacular Mountain Gap

Carved between two impressive mountain ranges, the road

through Franconia Notch is one of the most popular scenic drives in the East. You can enjoy several picturesque areas along this mountain drive.

Place: From Franconia, S on US 3 for 15 mi. to Lincoln; then S on I-93 for 15 mi.

Old Man of the Mountain

A visit to this natural stone profile of a man's face will be well worth your while. Created by five separate ledges of granite, this famous face can easily be seen from the east shore of Profile Lake.

Place: Profile Lake, W of US 3, N of Franconia Notch.

Gilford

Great Hiking

This beautiful setting, located in the densely wooded Gunstock Ski Area, offers several hiking trails —with wonderful views. Fresh woodland ponds provide ideal picnic spots.

Place: E of Laconia, 10 mi. off US 3 on NH 11A.
Contact: (603) 524-3286
Note: Fee for camping.

Gorham

White Birch Stands

The Shelburne white birches surround NH 16 for miles as you travel south of Gorham. In autumn, the fluttering leaves turn amber, creating a breathtaking drive.

Hampton

Trolley Exhibit

Many fascinating antiques are on display at the Tuck Memorial Museum, including toys, tools, documents—even an exhibit of old-fashioned trolley cars. In addition to the historical memorabilia, a one-room schoolhouse has been restored to recreate the feeling of an earlier day.

Time: July-Aug., Mon.-Sun., 1-4 p.m.; Sept.-June, by appt. only.

Place: 40 Park Ave., on Meeting House Green.
Contact: (603) 926-3395

Hanover

Dartmouth Concert Hall

The Hopkins Center for the Creative and Performing Arts is one of the most popular attractions for visitors to Dartmouth College. Housed in a building known for its architectural significance, the center includes the concert hall, theaters and art galleries. There's also a beautiful outdoor garden theater and sculpture court.

Time: Center: Sun.-Thurs., 7:30 a.m.-11 p.m.; Fri.-Sat., 7:30 a.m.-midnight. Tours: 9 a.m., 11 a.m. and 3 p.m.
Place: E of I-91 on NH 10.
Contact: (603) 646-2875

Hebron

Sculptured Rocks

On the north side of Newfound Lake are stunning sculptured rocks, one of the most interesting and popular geological tourist attractions in the state.

Place: N end of Newfound Lake, off NH 3A.

NEW HAMPSHIRE

Hillsboro

Truck Collection

For all trucking fans, Richard Kemp has created the diesel dream. He keeps his collection of more than 100 trucks on display at his home, including a 1930 original "Bulldog Mack," a 1916 "Selden" and a dozen old crawler trailers. For anyone who shares his interest in these snub-nosed machines, Mr. Kemp's yard is something to see!

Time: Anytime.
Place: On River St., 500 ft. from US 202.
Contact: (603) 464-3386
Note: The contact above is Mr. Kemp's home number; he'll be glad to talk to you if you're a real truck lover!

Jaffrey

Cathedral of the Pines

This nondenominational shrine is a memorable stop if you are in the area. Organ concerts are performed daily in this serene setting where memorials honor our nation's war dead.

Time: July-Aug., 9 a.m.-5 p.m.; May-June and Sept.-Oct., 9 a.m.-4 p.m. Organ concerts: mid-June-mid-Sept., Mon.- Thurs., 11 a.m.-12:30 p.m. and 1-3:30 p.m.
Place: 2 mi. S of town via NH 119 on Cathedral Rd.
Contact: (603) 899-3300

Keene

Main Street, USA

While visiting Keene, take a good look at Main Street. A full 172 feet across, the town boasts that its street is the widest in the world.

Scenic Picnic Stop

Nestled between wooded hills, the Chesterfield Gorge is the perfect scene for a picnic lunch. Or stop by this relaxing spot after a full day of sightseeing.

Place: Off NH 9, W of town.

Lincoln

Logging Contest

Learn about the exciting skills of the old lumber industry at the Annual Logging Championship Contest. Woodchopping, steeplechase and log rolling are just a few of the events that recreate this legendary time.

Time: Sept.
Place: E of I-93 on NH 112.
Contact: Marketing Department, Loon Mountain Recreation Corp., Lincoln, NH 03251; (603) 745-8111.

Manchester

State's Largest Public Art Museum

New Hampshire's largest public art museum is the Currier Gallery of Art. In addition to American paintings and antiques, it houses rare European paintings dating back to the 14th century. Make sure to see the collections of silver, glass and pewter.

Time: Tues., Wed., Fri., Sat., 10 a.m.-4 p.m.; Thurs., 10 a.m.-10 p.m.; Sun., 2-5 p.m.
Place: 192 Orange St.
Contact: (603) 669-6144

Local History

Experience the history of this region in the excellent collections of the Manchester Historic Association. Exhibits and displays recreate everyday life from Indian times to the present, including clothing, paintings and fine furniture.

Time: Tues.-Fri., 11 a.m.-4 p.m.; Sat., 10 a.m.-4 p.m.
Place: 129 Amherst St.
Contact: (603) 622-7531

Merrimack

Beer-Making

Take this informative 25-minute tour and learn all the steps that go into making and packaging beer. Anheuser-Busch also provides a Hospitality Room where visitors over 18 can sample the finished product.

Time: May-Oct., Mon.-Sat., 9:30 a.m.-3:30 p.m.; Sun., 11:30 a.m.-4 p.m. Nov.-Apr., Wed.-Sat., 9:30 a.m.-3:30 p.m.; Sun., 11:30 a.m.-3:30 p.m.
Place: 1000 Daniel Webster Hwy. (US 3), off Everett Turnpike.
Contact: (603) 889-6631

Clydesdale Horses

A visit to Merrimack means a visit to the wonderful Clydesdale horses at the Anheuser-Busch brewery. These "gentle giants" live in a replica of a

19th-century farm building that includes a carriage house, tack room and vintage wagons. There are always at least three of the big horses here along with displays on the history of the breed.

Time: May-Oct., Mon.-Sat., 9:30 a.m.-3:30 p.m.; Sun., 11:30 a.m.-4 p.m. Nov.-Apr., Wed.-Sat., 9:30 a.m.-3:30 p.m.; Sun., 11:30 a.m.-4 p.m.
Place: 1000 Daniel Webster Hwy. (US 3), off Everett Turnpike.
Contact: (603) 889-6631

New Castle

Fort of the Revolution

Few people realize the significant role that Fort Constitution played in the American Revolution. The museum and tours explain the exciting history of the fort, built in 1632, including a plot by Paul Revere and the Sons of Liberty to capture five tons of gunpowder from the British. A very important stop.

Time: Open year-round, daylight hours.
Place: 4 mi. E of Portsmouth on NH 1B.
Contact: (603) 271-3556

Portsmouth

River Rest Area

The highlight of a picnic at Prescott Park is the lovely riverbank setting among gardens and fountains. Enjoy the free amphitheater and the view from the fishing pier. After lunch, make your stop complete with a visit to the Sheafe Warehouse Museum (1705), featuring carved mastheads and ship models.

Time: Amphitheater: July-Aug. (check locally for times). Museum: late May-mid-June, Sat.-Sun., 10 a.m.-6 p.m.; mid-June-Labor Day, Mon.-Sun., 10 a.m.-6 p.m.
Place: Along Piscataqua River, from State St. to Mechanics St.
Contact: Chamber of Commerce: (603) 436-1118. Amphitheater: (603) 431-5846. Museum: (603) 436-1486.

Warren

Big Game Animal Display

Several species of big game African and Indian animals are exhibited at the Morse Museum—the prize trophies of the two Morse brothers. Stuffed and mounted animals, skins and safari mementos also fill the hall. Added attrac-

NEW HAMPSHIRE

Warren

tion is a unique collection of shoes from all over the world.
Time: Mem. Day-July 4, Sat.-Sun., 10 a.m.-5 p.m. July 4-Labor Day, Mon.-Sun., 10 a.m.-5 p.m.
Place: Along NH 25C, on Main St.
Contact: (603) 271-2666

Wolfeboro Center

Pewter Masters

Great care is taken at the Hampshire Pewter Company to make hand-crafted pewter of the finest quality. On the 20-minute tour you can see craftsmen making castings of molten pewter, using a 400-year old formula, and then hand-finishing them. Many of these pieces are displayed in museums around the country.
Time: Mon.-Fri., 9 a.m.-4 p.m., tours on the hour.
Place: NH 28 and NH 109.
Contact: (603) 569-4944

Statewide

Saltwater Fishing

New Hampshire has only 17 miles of coastline, so why not see it all? Saltwater fishing is great fun and requires no license except for smelt and clams. Some of the more tasty varieties available to the rod-and-reel set are tuna, mackerel, cod, haddock, harbor and sea pollock, coho salmon and flounder. Fishing is popular along piers and even from the rocky shoreline.
Contact: (603) 271-3421

Maple Syrup Industry

Nothing creates the essential feeling of New England better than a visit to a snowy maple orchard in the late winter or early spring. Several maple producers scattered across the state offer tours of their sugarhouses. Here you can see the sap being boiled into syrup. Some producers also offer "sugaring off" parties for a small fee, which are very informative and lots of fun. The contact below will send a free "Visitors' List" to you upon request; it lists the members of the state Maple Producers' Association that will give tours or sugaring parties.
Time: Early March-late Apr.
Contact: NH Dept. of Agriculture, 85 Manchester St., Park Plaza, Concord, NH 03301; (603) 271-3788.

NEW JERSEY

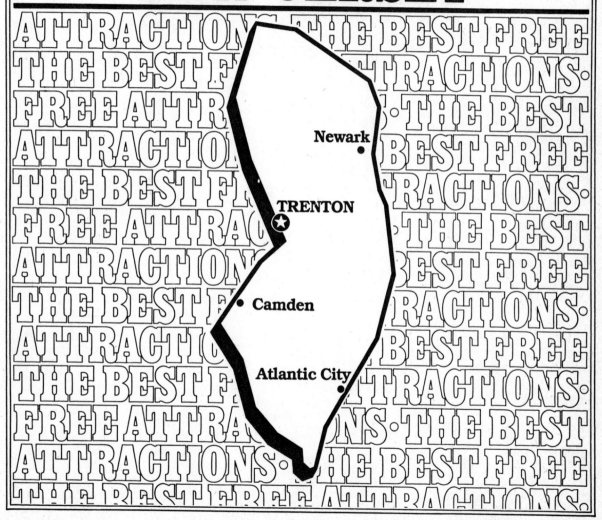

Newark

TRENTON

Camden

Atlantic City

NEW JERSEY

Absecon

Authentic German Winery

Gross's Highland Winery is the East's largest direct-to-the-consumer winery and is especially known for its fine champagne equipment. Visitors will see New Jersey wine made according to old European traditions and will get a chance to sample the results in a hospitality room.

Time: Mon.-Sat., 9 a.m.-6 p.m.; groups of over 25 by reservation only.
Place: Take NJ 561 5 mi. NW of Atlantic City to 212 Jim Leeds Rd.
Contact: Gross's Highland Winery, 212 Jim Leeds Rd., Absecon, NJ 08201; (609) 652-1187.

Asbury Park

Band Concerts

Enjoy summer band music under the stars at the Arthur Pryor Memorial Pavilion in Asbury Park. An adjoining convention hall features visiting celebrities.
Contact: (201) 775-0900

Atlantic City

World's Oldest Boardwalk

Atlantic City's most famous attraction might very well be its six and a half-mile boardwalk, built in 1870 as the first of its kind in the world. Free beach facilities are also in the vicinity.
Contact: (609) 345-7536

A Safe Bet

It doesn't cost anything to watch roulette wheels spin and blackjack being dealt. But if you want to do any more than that, plan to spend some money. Atlantic City has six casinos, all complete with hotel, restaurant and bar facilities. Admission to the gambling rooms is free.
Contact: Atlantic City Convention and Visitors Bureau, 16 Central Pier, Atlantic City, NJ 08401; (609) 345-3305.

Garden Pier

Located along the famous boardwalk, this amusement pier is home of the Atlantic City Art Center. Free concerts are also offered here in an outdoor amphitheatre.
Time: Art Center: 9 a.m.-4 p.m. Concerts: July-Aug., Sun., Mon. and Wed., 7-8:30 p.m.
Place: Boardwalk and New Jersey Ave.
Contact: (609) 348-7044

Miss America Parade

Stunning floats and lovely queen candidates highlight this gala parade held each year as part of Atlantic City's renowned Miss America Pageant.
Contact: (609) 345-7571

Basking Ridge

Wildlife Refuge

More than 200 species of wildlife frequent the 13 square miles of marsh, grassland, oak and beech trees that comprise the Great Swamp National Wildlife Refuge. Interpretation is available at Somerset Environmental Education Center.
Time: Headquarters: Mon.-Fri., 8 a.m.-4:30 p.m. Trails and information booth: dawn-dusk.
Place: 1 mi N of town on US 202, then 2 mi. E on Madisonville Rd., 1.5 mi. NE on Lee's Hill Rd., then right on Long Hill Rd.
Contact: R.D. 1, P.O. Box 148, Basking Ridge, NJ 07920; (201) 647-1222.

Branchville

Peters Valley

A group of historic buildings in the Delaware Water Gap

National Recreation Area serve as studios for area craftsmen. See these artisans at work and examine their displays. Weavers, woodworkers, jewelrymakers, ceramicists and blacksmiths are featured.

Time: Apr.-Dec., Tues.-Sat., 1-4 p.m.
Place: 8 mi. NW of town via US 206, Cty. Rd. 521, then S on Cty. Rd. 615.
Contact: (201) 948-5202

Stokes State Forest

Situated on the Kittatinny Ridge, this 15,000-acre forest features some of the most scenic mountain country in New Jersey. Particularly picturesque are the views from Sunrise Mountain. Tillman Ravine, a natural gorge, is the southern corner of the park. Hiking, picnicking, hunting and fishing facilities are available.

Place: 3 mi. N of town on US 206.
Contact: (201) 948-3820

Bridgeton

Glass and Iron Collection

Located in the original 1815 office of Cumberland Nail and Iron Works, Bridgeton's earliest industry, the Nail Mill Office Museum features a collection of southern New Jersey glass and iron.

Time: Mon.-Fri., 9 a.m.-4 p.m.; Sat., 11 a.m.-4 p.m.; Sun., 2-5 p.m.; closed holidays.
Place: 1 Mayor Aitken Dr.
Contact: (609) 455-4100

Woodruff Indian Museum

Some 20,000 Lenni Lenape Indian artifacts up to 10,000 years old are featured in this museum in the Bridgeton City Library. Among the items on display are clay pots, pipes and implements.

Time: Sept.-June, Mon.-Sat., 1-4 p.m.; July-Aug., Mon.-Fri., 1-4 p.m. Other times and groups, reservations required.
Place: 150 E. Commerce St.
Contact: (609) 451-2620

Burlington

Birthplace of James Fenimore Cooper

Originally settled by Quakers in 1677, Burlington is the former capital of West Jersey. Many of its quaint buildings are exactly as they were in colonial times, including the birthplace of James Fenimore Cooper, which dates back to 1780.

Place: Off NJ 130 and I-295.
Contact: (609) 386-3993

Camden

Walt Whitman House

The famous poet lived in this Victorian Row House from 1873-1892. This state shrine contains original furnishings and other mementos.

Time: Thurs.-Sat., 9 a.m.-noon and 1-6 p.m.; Sun., 1-6 p.m. May-Aug., Wed., noon-5 p.m. and 6-8 p.m. Sept.-Apr., Wed., 9 a.m.-noon and 1-5 p.m.
Place: 330 Mickle St., off US 30 between 3rd and 4th Sts.
Contact: (609) 964-5383

Soup Bowl Museum

Three centuries' worth of the most elegant soup bowls and tureens are not your usual museum fare. But what else would you expect from the Campbell (soup) Museum? Over 250 objects from 24 countries are on display, including pieces dating from 500 B.C. Some of these elaborate silver, porcelain and china soup bowls were used by European royalty during the 1700s.

Time: Mon.-Fri., 9:30 a.m.-5 p.m.
Place: Campbell Place, just off US 30.
Contact: (609) 964-4000

Cape May

Oldest Seashore Resort

Founded in 1685, Cape May is the nation's oldest seashore resort. In the Victorian part of the city many of the old homes and hotels, popular when it was the most important shore resort in the country, have been restored. The Cape May Court House on Route 9 contains an historic museum, park and zoo.
Contact: (609) 465-7181

Clam Shell Pitching Contest

On the weekend before Labor Day weekend, Cape May engages in its annual clam shell pitching contest at Steger's Beach. The purpose of this sport is to pitch clam shells 25 feet into a three-inch hole dug into hard-packed sand. Judges award points to the shells that come closest to the hole.
Time: Weekend before Labor Day weekend, Sat.-Sun., 10 a.m.
Place: Steger's Beach.
Contact: (609) 465-7181

False Diamonds

This small coastal town on the tip of New Jersey's peninsula is one of the oldest seashore resorts on the Atlantic Coast and has many 19th-century structures still intact. It is particularly known for its deposits of quartz pebbles known as "Cape May Diamonds," which can be found on the beach at Cape May Point.
Contact: (609) 886-0901

Chester

Historic Village

History left its imprint on the quaint town of Chester during two eras. In Revolutionary War times, Chester was a stage-coach stop on a line that ran from Philadelphia to New York City, and many of its buildings were constructed in that era. After the Civil War, iron was mined near the town, and many of the miners' homes remain. Now, Chester is the haunt of amateur historians. Take a walking tour of the town. The public house, a tavern built in the early 1800s, is on the National Register of Historic Sites. Many miners' homes are now occupied by small shops.
Time: Walking tours: anytime.
Place: Throughout town.
Contact: (201) 879-6366

Elwood

Glass Blowing

Glass cutting and blowing demonstrations are featured at Messina Glass and China Inc., the country's biggest retailer of Noritake china.
Time: Call contact for hours, which vary seasonally.
Place: Downtown on US 30.
Contact: (609) 561-1474

Englishtown

Auction

The popular Englishtown Auction features a 25-acre flea market, 700 vendors, various antiques, produce, clothing and other new and used merchandise.

Place: Wilson Ave., jct. of NJ 522 and 527.
Contact: (201) 446-9644

Far Hills

Golf Museum

Golfers will love this—a history of golf in pictures and trophies is featured in the Golf House of the United States Golf Association in Far Hills.

Time: Mon.-Fri., 9 a.m.-5 p.m.; Sat.-Sun., 10 a.m.-4 p.m.
Place: On Cty. Rd. 512, 2 mi. E of jct. with US 202.
Contact: (201) 234-2300

Fort Lee

Historic Park

Constructed on the site of the gun batteries and magazines of Fort Lee, this 33-acre park features a revolutionary period museum, tours and a panoramic view of the Hudson River and New York skyline. Picnic facilities and historic hiking trails are also available.

Time: Wed.-Sun., 9 a.m.-sunset.
Place: Hudson Terrace.
Contact: (201) 461-3956
Note: Parking fee on weekends.

Fort Monmouth

Military Museum

The US Army Signal Corps Museum at Fort Monmouth is one of the largest military and technological centers devoted to training, research and development in communications and automatic data processing systems. Displays reveal the development of military communication from smoke signals and carrier pigeons to the present day.

Time: Mon.-Fri., 8 a.m.-4 p.m.
Place: Myer Hall, Ave. of Memories.
Contact: (201) 532-9000
Note: Children under 14 must be with an adult.

Hackettstown

Large Fish Farm

The 300-acre Hayford State Fish Hatchery is one of the nation's largest fish farms. It is literally teeming with millions of trout, bass, bluegill and sunfish, which are raised for stocking in state rivers and lakes.

Time: Mon.-Fri., 8 a.m.-4:30 p.m.; Sat.-Sun., 8 a.m.-6 p.m.
Place: Hatchery Rd., 1 mi. S of US 46.
Contact: (201) 852-3676
Note: Tours by appt.

Haddonfield

Indian King Tavern

The Indian King Tavern, an old bar and inn, is being restored to the way it may have appeared when it was built in 1750. Only guided tours are offered.

Time: Tours: Wed.-Fri., 9-11:30 a.m., 1-5:30 p.m.; Sat., 10-11:30 a.m., 1-5:30 p.m.; Sun., 1-5:30 p.m.
Place: 233 E. Kings Hwy.
Contact: (609) 429-6792
Note: No groups larger than 10 are allowed.

Highlands

Twin Lights State Historic Site

This historic sight on the Jersey shore was built in 1862 to guide ships into New York harbor. Visit the fine marine museum on the site.

Time: Late-May-Labor Day, 9 a.m.-5 p.m.; closed on Mon.
Place: Just N of town, off NJ 36.
Contact: (201) 872-9712

Sandy Hook Recreation Area

The Sandy Hook section of the Gateway National Recreation Area is one of the first stops for travelers heading south to the Jersey shore. In addition to swimming and fishing, there

NEW JERSEY

Highlands

are nice areas to picnic or to take a self-guided walk or guided tour. Since the area is still being developed, you should ask for more information at the Information Center.
Time: Information Center: 8 a.m.-5 p.m. Recreation Area: sunrise-sunset. Tour hours vary by season; call ahead.
Place: 5 mi. E of Atlantic Highlands on NJ 36.
Contact: P.O. Box 437, Highlands, NJ 07732; (201) 872-0092.

Hoboken
Model Shipbuilding
The building and sailing of model ships is a featured attraction of the fascinating Marine Laboratory on the campus of Stevens Institute of Technology in Hoboken.
Place: Hudson St.
Contact: (201) 420-5100

Jackson
Rova Farms
A piece of pre-revolutionary Russia is preserved in Rova Farm Resort, where a Russian Orthodox priest demonstrates gold and silver work, icon painting and Ukrainian Easter egg decorating. The commun-

ity was started in the 1920s by Russian immigrants. It now has two churches, including St. Vladimir's, which is elaborately decorated with mosaics. Each year on the last Sunday in July, thousands gather for the St. Vladimir's Day feast. Tours are free, though a donation is requested. (Admission to the feast is free too, though you must pay to be fed!)
Time: Tours by appt.
Place: Cty. 571 in town.
Contact: (201) 928-0928

Margate

Lucy the Elephant
Lucy is a 100-year-old building shaped like a huge elephant.

She stands six stories tall, weighs 90 tons, is sculpted from nearly a million pieces of wood and is covered by a tin skin. She was originally built in 1881 as an attraction to draw prospective land buyers. Restoration of her interior was completed in 1977 and today she is designated as a National Historic Landmark. A museum and gift shop are nearby.
Time: Jan.-mid-Sept., 10 a.m.-5 p.m. Subject to change.
Place: 9200 Atlantic Ave., take the Garden State Parkway exit 36 to Rt. 563.
Contact: (609) 823-6473

Morristown
Foster Fields Farm
A two-story Gothic Revival farmhouse is the centerpiece of the Foster Fields Living Historic Farm, a gentleman's farm restored to the way it looked in the 1880s. A film shown at the visitor center shows farming methods of that era, and a small museum has farm implements of that time. When restoration work is complete, there will be cattle and crops on the spread.
Time: May-Oct., Sat., 10 a.m.-5 p.m.; Sun., noon-5 p.m.
Place: 1 mi. W of town on NJ 24.
Contact: (201) 285-6688

Millville

World's Largest Holly Farm

The world's largest holly orchard, containing over 4,000 holly trees, can be found at American Holly Products Inc. in Millville. The Holly House, located in the center of the orchard, includes a museum with a huge collection of holly-motif china, plus wood carvings, painting and furniture made from holly. Small holly plants are sold.

Time: Jan.-Mar. and June-Oct., Mon.-Fri., 8 a.m.-4 p.m. Sept.-Oct., Sat., 8 a.m.-4 p.m. Apr.-May and Nov.-Dec., 8 a.m.-4 p.m. Closed holidays.
Place: 5 mi. W of town via NJ 49.
Contact: (609) 825-4595

Newark

Cherry Blossoms

In mid-April, Newark offers a stunning display of Oriental flowering cherry trees in Branch Brook Park. It's said that this display surpasses even those in Washington DC's Tidal Basin. At night, the trees are floodlighted, inviting strollers.

Contact: (201) 733-6454

Ocean City

Crab Race and Beauty Pageant

Each August in Ocean City is highlighted by the world's only Hermit Tree Crab Beauty Pageant. Entrants compete for the coveted title of Miss Crustacean USA. The beauty contest is followerd by the World's Championship Hermit Tree Crab Race in which contestants shoulder each other for the Cucumber Rind Cup. Theme of the event is "Shellfish Can Be Beautiful," and competitors are often decorated in colorful shells and fancy costumes.

Place: 12th St. Beach.
Contact: P.O. Box 174, Ocean City, NJ 08226; (609) 399-6111.

Band Concerts

Summer visitors to Ocean City can be entertained every night by band concerts on the Music Pier. Sometimes these melodious interludes are accompanied by colorful fireworks displays.

Contact: (609) 399-2629

Palisades

Palisades Interstate Parks

This 78,914-acre system of conservation and recreation areas along the west side of the Hudson River includes Bear Mountain and Harriman State Parks (New York) and Fort Lee Historical Park (New Jersey). The parks feature an abundance of picnic areas, fishing, boating and swimming facilities and scenic nature trails and drives. The towering cliffs of the Palisades along the Hudson River in New Jersey were a popular movie setting from 1907 to 1916.

Time: Trailside Museum at Bear Mountain: 9 a.m.-5 p.m.
Place: Via Palisades Interstate Pkwy., starting at New Jersey end of George Washington Bridge; then US 9W, NJ/NY 17 and US 9 to Bear Mountain Bridge, Dewey Thruway exit 13.
Contact: (914) 786-2701
Note: There are fees for parking and for some activities.

Point Pleasant

Beni Hana Grand Prix

Activities at this week-long event are attended by about a

NEW JERSEY

Point Pleasant

quarter million people and include the largest off-shore powerboat race in the world plus a beauty pageant, parade and fireworks.
Contact: (201) 899-2424

Inner-Tube Race

An inner-tube race caps off a weekend of arts and crafts at Point Pleasant. Contestants

line up on the beach, blow up their tubes, jump into the ocean and flail toward a finish line 100 yards away. (To enter requires a sponsor; to watch is free.) On the day before the race, townspeople close the

center of the community to traffic and hold an arts and crafts fair attended by people and artisans from all over the region.
Time: Race: usually the 3rd Sun. in Sept. Fair is held the day before.
Place: Point Pleasant Beach.
Contact: (201) 899-2424

Powerboats

Sometimes more than a million people gather on Point Pleasant Beach to watch one of the biggest powerboat races in the country. The big boats race on the waves of the Atlantic just off shore.
Time: 3rd Wed. of July.
Place: Point Pleasant Beach.
Contact: (201) 899-2424

Princeton

Princeton University

Students will guide you through the 2,500 acre, ivy-walled campus of Princeton University to such attractions as art and natural history museums, a two-million volume library and sculptures by Calder, Lipchitz, Moore, Nevelson and Picasso. Woodrow Wilson was president of the University from 1902 to 1910 and the Woodrow Wilson School of Public and Interna-

tional Affairs is named in his honor.
Time: Mon.-Sat., 9 a.m.-5 p.m.; Sun., 1-5 p.m. Campus tours: Mon.-Sat., 10 and 11:30 a.m. and 1:30 and 3:30 p.m., except holidays or during scheduled events.
Place: In Princeton, off NJ 1 and NJ 206.
Contact: (609) 452-3000 or 452-3603

Bainbridge House

This restored 18th-century residence features two period rooms, a library, photo archives, special exhibits and a children's museum room.
Time: Tues.-Fri., 10 a.m.-4 p.m.; Sat.-Sun., 2-4 p.m.
Place: 158 Nassau St.
Contact: (609) 921-7676

Saddle River

Bee Farm

Myron Surmach, 85-year-old owner of his own apiary on West Saddle River Road, will show you around the farm and explain about bees, beekeeping and honey. As a special treat, taste the special Ukrainian-style honey or buy some raw honey at the apiary store to take home.
Time: Apr.-Oct., Tues.,-Sat., 10 a.m.-4 p.m. Please call a few days in advance.
Place: 169 W. Saddle River Rd.

Contact: Myron Surmach's Apiary, 169 W. Saddle River Rd., Saddle River, NJ 07458; (201) 327-6072.

Salem

Hancock House

This is the only house still standing in New Jersey in which a massacre occurred during the Revolutionary War. It served as a barracks during the American Revolution and was attacked in 1778 by 300 soldiers armed with bayonets. Restoration includes period furnishings.

Time: Wed.-Fri., 9 a.m.-noon and 1-6 p.m.; Sat., 10 a.m.-noon and 1-6 p.m.; Sun., 1-6 p.m.
Place: 5 mi. S of town via NJ 49 to Hancock's Bridge Rd. in Hancock's Bridge.
Contact: (609) 935-4373

Scotch Plains

Watchung Reservation

A 575-foot high observation tower highlights the attractions on the Watchung Reservation, a 2,000-acre wooded area in the Watchung Mountains. Also featured are picnic areas, nature trails, fishing and ice-skating facilities, playgrounds, riding trails and a ten-acre nursery and rhododendron display garden.

Place: SW of town off Rte. 527.
Contact: Union County Dept. of Parks and Recreation, P.O. Box 275, Elizabeth, NJ 07207; (201) 232-5930.

Seaside Heights

Seaside Heights

Summer is packed with activities in Seaside Heights, including parades, fireworks and a Mardi Gras on the weekend after Labor Day. There are also miles of boardwalk to see any time of year.

Contact: (201) 793-9100

Smithville

Restored 18th-Century Town

Smithville is a restored 18th-century southern New Jersey town containing 45 period buildings—these include a gristmill, chapel and federal homes. There are also many commercial shops and restaurants. The Old Village has a 19th-century oystering vessel floating on the town pond.

Time: Shops: May-Sept., 11 a.m.-9 p.m.; rest of year, Mon.-Fri., 11 a.m.-5 p.m., Sat., 11 a.m.-9 p.m., Sun., 11 a.m.-7 p.m. Old Village: daylight hours.

Place: At the jct. of US 9 and Cty. Rd. 561A, 12 mi. N of Atlantic City.
Contact: (609) 652-7777

Sussex

Appalachian Walking Trail

Entering New Jersey along the New York border, this portion of the famous cross-country Appalachian Trail runs eastward along the apex of the state's northern mountains, reaching its peak at High Point State Park, 1,821 feet high. It then turns south, traveling the tops of the Kittatiny Ridge and finally coming "down to earth" at Delaware Water Gap, where it crosses into Pennsylvania over the Delaware River.

Contact: (609) 292-2733

Trenton

Planetarium

One of the few Intermediate Space Transit planetaria in the world, the New Jersey State Museum Planetarium features changing programs with emphasis on the concepts that have become important in current space probes. Traditional shows, public observing field

Trenton

trips and children's programs are all free.

Time: Shows: Sat.-Sun., 2, 3 and 4 p.m. Public observing: Apr.-May and Oct.-Nov., Fri., 8:30 p.m.
Place: 205 W. State St.
Contact: (609) 292-6333
Note: No children under 7 except for special children's programs, July-Aug., Fri., 10 a.m. and at other times around Christmas and Easter. Tickets available half hour in advance.

Statewide

Garden State Parkway Scenic Drive

The drive along the Garden State Parkway is one of the most scenic in the state. Cut out of the wilderness, the parkway runs from New York to the tip of New Jersey by Cape May and includes views of the ocean, wayside stops and rest areas.
Contact: (609) 292-2470

NEW YORK

Buffalo

⭐ ALBANY

New York

NEW YORK

Akron

Making Gum

Stop in to see the people at the Ford Gum and Machine Co.—they're the ones who stock the ubiquitous gum-ball machine. The sight of the finished product will set your mouth to watering!

Time: Mon.-Fri., 10:30 a.m.
Place: Newton and Hoag Aves.
Contact: (716) 542-4561

Albany

Empire State Plaza

The Gov. Nelson A. Rockefeller Empire State Plaza, topping Albany's skyline, is a huge cluster of public buildings. Here you'll find the Swan Street Building, the Justice Building, the Legislative Office Building, the Convention Center and the Performing Arts Center, which includes a 987-seat theater and a 500-seat recital hall.

Time: Tours: 9 a.m.-4 p.m., on the hour.
Place: Madison Ave. and S. Swan St.
Contact: (518) 474-2418

State Capitol

Take an hour-long tour of the New York State Capitol, a French Renaissance building begun in 1868 and finished 30 years later at a cost of $25 million. Gardens and fountains surround this elaborately finished building.

Time: 9 a.m.-4 p.m.
Place: On top of State St. Hill.
Contact: (518) 474-2418

Hudson Valley Life

The exhibits of the Albany Institute of History and Art highlight the history of the Upper Hudson Valley and its settlement. There also are many fine displays of contemporary art.

Time: Tues.-Sat., 10 a.m.-4:45 p.m.; Sun., 2-5 p.m.
Place: 125 Washington Ave.
Contact: (518) 463-4478

Bristol Springs

Observatory

Look through an observatory telescope at the planets, stars and other heavenly objects. The C. E. K. Mees Observatory, run by the University of Rochester, is higher in altitude than any other observatory in the East.

Time: May-Sept., Sat.-Sun., after sunset.
Place: NY 64 just S of town.
Contact: (716) 275-4385

Buffalo

Downtown View

From the observation tower on the 28th floor of the Buffalo City Hall, you can get a 360-degree view of the city and the surrounding area.

Time: Mon.-Fri., 9:30 a.m.-3:30 p.m.; Sat., 9 a.m.-5 p.m.
Place: Niagara Sq. on Delaware Ave.
Contact: (716) 856-4200, ext. 342

Art Gallery

The primary attraction in the Albright-Knox Art Gallery is its collection of 20th-century art—painting and sculpture. It also has pieces dating to 3000 B.C. The older exhibits represent Egyptian, Classical, Pre-Columbian, Sumerian and African art.

Time: Tues.-Sat., 10 a.m.-5 p.m.; Sun., noon-5 p.m.
Place: 1285 Elmwood Ave.
Contact: (716) 882-8700

Science Museum

Contemplate something as down to earth as a flower or as abstract as the size of the universe. The Buffalo Museum of Science covers these and many things in between. The Hall of Plant Life features wildflowers and other plants. In other halls you'll see birds, animals, insects, reptiles and fossils. In the Hall of the Universe, exhibits demonstrate or explain the awesome dimensions and workings of space, stars and other celestial subjects.

Time: Sept.-May, 10 a.m.-5 p.m.; Fri., 10 a.m.-10 p.m.; holidays, 1:30-5:30 p.m.
Place: Near Kensington Expressway (NY 33) and Best St.
Contact: (716) 896-5200

Canandaigua

Race Track

Feed sugar and apples to thoroughbred horses at the Finger Lakes Race Track. Here you'll learn about the horses and how they are cared for. Make

reservations at least a week in advance.
Time: June-Aug., Tues., Wed. and Fri. mornings.
Place: On NY 96, E of NY 332 and S of Thruway exit 44.
Contact: P.R. Dept.: (716) 924-3232.

Castile

Maple Syrup

See how the people working on the family-run Apple Hill Farm make maple syrup on a large scale. Syrup is collected from 3,000 maple-tree taps and is then run by plastic tubing to two gas evaporators.
Time: Early Mar.-Apr., 8 a.m.-5:30 p.m.
Place: .5 mi. S of town on NY 19A.
Contact: (716) 493-2398

East Bethany

Fossil Beds

In constructing the railroad near East Bethany, workers cut into a hill and exposed layers of fossilized rock. Embedded in the outcrops are Upper Devonian brachiopods, mollusks, trilobites and parts of crinoids. The looking is best when the rock is wet—in the spring or after a rain. Watch out for trains!
Place: 2 mi. N of NY 20 on Bethany Center Rd.

East Bloomfield

Cat's Whisker

Listen to early radio on a "cat's whisker" crystal set. See more than 25,000 radio and electronics items on display at the Antique Wireless Association Electronic Communications Museum, one of only two museums in the country devoted solely to electronics history. One of the exhibits is a 1925 radio store.
Time: May-Oct., Wed., 7-9 p.m.; Sun., 2-5 p.m.
Place: Village Park in town.
Contact: (716) 657-7489

Fairport

Lollypop Farm

Deer, burros, goats, llamas, sheep and calves—more than 150 animals and birds in all—can be seen at the Humane Society Lollypop Farm. This attraction is especially interesting to children.
Time: 10 a.m.-5 p.m.
Place: 99 Victor Rd.
Contact: (716) 223-1330

Goshen

Trotting Track

The harness-racing track at Goshen is the oldest track still operating in the country and

NEW YORK

Goshen

the only one that is a National Historical Landmark. The Hall of Fame of the Trotter Museum features Currier and Ives lithographs, wood carvings, dioramas, bronze statues and horse-racing films.
Time: Mon.-Sat., 10 a.m.-5 p.m.; Sun., 1:30-5 p.m.
Place: 240 Main St.
Contact: (914) 294-6330

Haines Falls

Highest Falls

Kaaterskill Falls, the highest waterfall in New York, plunges 180 feet over one ledge and 80 feet over a second lip. It is one of the most frequently depicted scenes in early New York landscape art. Trails from North Lake State Park wind up around the falls and invite hikers.
Time: Anytime.
Place: In town on NY 23A.
Contact: (518) 622-3204

Hamlin

Barge Canal Trail

A hiking and biking trail now being built along the old New York State Barge Canal will eventually link Albany and Buffalo, a distance of about 300 miles. You'll be able to see pleasure boats on the canal, scenic woods and pasture. Only sections of the trail are finished now—about 80 miles in all. For more information call or write the contact below.
Contact: New York State Office of Parks and Recreation, Empire State Plaza, Albany, NY 12238; (518) 474-0414.

Hammondsport

Taylor Wine

Take a bus tour of New York's well-known Taylor Wine Co. You can see the grape-crushing equipment that has replaced bare human feet. Glass tubes carry off the grape juice to where it will ferment and age. On your way out, taste samples of this renowned wine and down some hot hors d'oeuvres.
Time: July-Oct., Mon.-Sat., 10 a.m.-4 p.m.; Sun., noon-4 p.m. Rest of year, Mon.-Fri., 11 a.m.-3 p.m.
Place: Cty. Rd. 88, 1.5 mi. S of town.
Contact: (607) 569-2111

Highland Falls

West Point

One of the country's biggest collections of military artifacts is right where you would expect to find it—the museum at the US Military Academy at West Point. Among the many buildings open to the public are the Old Cadet Chapel, the Chapel of the Most Holy Trinity and Fort Clinton. Start your self-guided tour with a film at the visitor center.
Time: Visitor center: Apr. 1-Dec. 31, 8:30 a.m.-4:30 p.m.; rest of year, Wed.-Sun., 8:30 a.m.-4:30 p.m.
Place: Off NY 218, in town.
Contact: Visitor Information Center, US Military Academy, West Point, NY 10996; (914) 938-2638 or 3507.

Ithaca

Herbert F. Johnson Museum

Designed by renowned architect I. M. Pei, this museum stands on the edge of Cornell University's campus and overlooks downtown Ithaca and the Cayuga Lake valley. Of special interest is the fine Oriental art collection on the top floor, where you'll also be treated to a panoramic view of the city.
Time: Tues.-Sun., 10 a.m.-5 p.m.
Place: Across from White Hall, on Cornell University's campus.
Contact: (607) 256-6464

Cornell Campus and Gorge

The Cornell campus is noted both for its Gothic and Romanesque architecture and for its magnificent setting on a hill overlooking Ithaca and Cayuga Lake. Even more inspiring are the two deep gorges which flank the campus.

Contact: (607) 256-1000

Sapsucker Sanctuary

Here's a challenge: try to identify the bird calls on a recording at the Sapsucker Woods Bird Sanctuary. There are some 30,000 separate calls! The Observatory overlooks a 10-acre pond where ducks, geese and other water birds lurk. Four miles of trail run through a woods filled with wildflowers in the spring.

Time: Sanctuary: anytime. Observatory: Mon.-Thur., 8 a.m.-5 p.m.; Fri., 8 a.m.-4:30 p.m.; Sat-Sun., 10 a.m.-5 p.m.
Place: 159 Sapsucker Woods Rd.
Contact: (607) 256-6200

Lodi

Silver Thread Falls

Tucked in a gorge near Lodi Point is 167-foot Silver Thread Falls. To see it, drive to the park near the railroad tracks on County Rd. 136 and walk south a quarter-mile to the railroad bridge. From there you can see the falls. To stand beneath it, drive to Lower Lake Road south of Lodi Point. Hike through the woods for a mile, and then walk upstream until you stand beneath the falling water.

Naples

Widmer's Wine Cellars

You get a few complimentary nips of wine after a tour of this noted wine seller. Widmer's Wine Cellars, Inc. also presents a slide show about wine.

Time: June-Oct., Mon.-Sat., 10 a.m.-3:30 p.m.; Sun., noon-4:30 p.m.
Place: West Ave., just N of town.
Contact: (716) 374-6311

Newark

Clock Museum

More than 100 clocks—some old, some new—are on display at the Hoffman Clock Museum. Some were painstakingly made by hand; others were rolled off assembly lines.

Time: July-Aug., Mon.-Fri., 9:30 a.m.-5:30 p.m. and 7-9 p.m.; rest of year, same hours and Sat., 9:30 a.m.-5:30 p.m.
Place: High St.
Contact: (315) 331-4370

Newburgh

Washington's Headquarters

A lock of George Washington's hair is in the museum at the Washington's Headquarters State Historic Site. The mainstay of the museum, however, are exhibits of Colonial life and the revolutionary war. Nearby is the Hasbrouck House, a Dutch-style building that was Washington's headquarters from April 1782 until August 1783.

Time: Apr.-Dec., Wed.-Sun., 9 a.m.-5 p.m.; Jan.-March, Sat.-Sun., 9 a.m.-5 p.m.
Place: Liberty and Washington Sts.
Contact: (914) 562-1195

New York City

African-American Institute

Drawings, etchings, sculpture, paintings and tapestries are some of the changing exhibits to be found in the African-American Institute. Call before you visit: the gallery closes between exhibitions.

Time: Mon.-Fri., 9 a.m.-5 p.m.; Sat., 11 a.m.-5 p.m.
Place: 833 United Nations Plaza (47th St. and First Ave.).
Contact: (212) 949-5666

New York

The History of Money

The American Numismatic Society has a large collection of US coins in good condition. It also has odd, rare or old forms of currency. One example is Chinese knife money, which fits all three categories.

Time: Tues.-Sat., 9:30 a.m.-4:30 p.m.
Place: 155th St. and Broadway.
Contact: (212) 234-3130

Challenge for Chickens

Though you have to pay to match wits with a chicken, it doesn't cost anything to watch

other people make fools of themselves. A chicken at the Arcade has been trained to play tic-tac-toe with the aid of a computer. The chicken is reported to be good! Another chicken dances—no brains, just another pretty face.

Time: Mon.-Thur., 10 a.m.-midnight; Fri.-Sun., 10 a.m.-2 a.m.
Place: 8 Mott St.
Contact: (212) 964-1542

Asia Gallery

Paintings, sculpture, ceramics and prints from China, India, Tibet, Ceylon, Nepal, Southeast Asia and Japan make up the Rockefeller collection at the Asia House Gallery. The exhibits range from contemporary back to more than 2,000 years old.

Time: Tues.-Sat., 10 a.m.-5 p.m.; Sun., 1-5 p.m.
Place: 725 Park Ave.
Contact: (212) 751-3210

Barnes and Noble

Professional puppeteers present children's shows at Barnes and Noble bookstore. They use all kinds of puppets—from hand puppets to marionettes—to present animated fairy tales. Sometimes there is a magic show instead.

Time: Sun., 11 a.m., 12:30 p.m.
Place: 126 Fifth Ave.
Contact: (212) 675-5500

Battery Park

From Battery Park at the south end of Manhattan, you get a sweeping view of the harbor and the Statue of Liberty. This is the launching point for the Staten Island Ferry. Sometimes there are special programs in the park.

Time: Anytime.
Place: End of Broadway at south tip of Manhattan.
Contact: (212) 269-0320

Bible House

Fragments of the Dead Sea Scrolls, replicas of the vessels in which they were found, a replica of the Gutenberg press and a replica of the Gutenberg Bible are on display at the Bible House. You must have four in your tour group and make reservations.

Time: Mon.-Fri., 9 a.m.-4:30 p.m.
Place: 1865 Broadway (at 61st St.).
Contact: (212) 581-7400

Boxing Hall of Fame

If you're really interested in boxing, if you knew who Roberto Duran was before he fought Sugar Ray Leonard, if you remember whom John L. Sullivan lost his title to, and if you watch every boxing match you can, you may go for the Boxing Hall of Fame. The exhibits are shown in the offices of *Ring* Magazine. There are plaster casts of the fists of Joe Louis, Muhammad Ali, Joe Frazier and other champions. There is the bell used in James "Boilermaker" Jeffry's fights. There are hundreds of photos. And more. A lot more.

Time: Mon.-Fri., 10 a.m.-5 p.m.
Place: 120 W. 31st St., sixth floor.
Contact: (212) 736-7464

Dramatic Softball

If you want to see your favorite Broadway star somewhere other than on a stage, drop by and watch the Broadway Stars' Softball League in action.

Time: Summer; times vary.
Place: Central Park.
Contact: (212) 360-8196

Bronx Zoo

In the World of Darkness at the Bronx Zoo, you will get a rare chance to see nocturnal animals going about their nighttime routines. There also is an African Plains section, where you will be separated from the wild animals of Africa only by a moat. In another part of the zoo, children can pet domesticated animals.

Time: Free Tues.-Thur., 10 a.m.-4:30 p.m.
Place: SW part of Bronx Park.
Contact: (212) 220-5100

Brooklyn Botanical Garden

The conservatory at the Brooklyn Botanical Garden has a variety of environments—the Tropical House, the Bonsai House (with miniature trees), the Fern House, the Cactus House and more.

Time: Conservatory: Tues.-Fri., 10 a.m.-4 p.m. Outdoor gardens: Oct.-March, Tues.-Fri., 8 a.m.-4:30 p.m.; Sat.-Sun., 10 a.m.-4:30 p.m. Rest of year, Tues.-Fri., 8 a.m.-6 p.m.; Sat.-Sun., 10 a.m.-6 p.m.
Place: 1000 Washington Ave.
Contact: (212) 622-4433

Brooklyn Bridge

New York, of course, is the home of the Brooklyn Bridge. And, of course, it is open for public display. Completed in 1883, it was one of the century's great accomplishments in engineering. By walking across it, you get a fine view of lower Manhattan. Just don't let anyone talk you into buying it.

Brooklyn Children's Zoo

Children who visit the Brooklyn Children's Zoo find themselves in an enchanted world of diamond crystals large enough to play in, domestic

animals they can touch and mechanical exhibits they can manipulate. They can also pit their tic-tac-toe skills against those of a computer.

Time: Mon., Wed.-Fri., 1-5 p.m.; Sat.-Sun., 10 a.m.-5 p.m.
Place: 145 Brooklyn Ave., on corner near St. Mark's Ave.
Contact: (212) 735-4432

Brooklyn Museum

Collections of Egyptian, classical and African art are the strong suits of the Brooklyn Museum. There are also rooms that are furnished like Colonial homes. Free concerts, lectures and movies are scheduled at various times.

Time: Wed.-Sat., 10 a.m.-5 p.m.; Sun., noon-5 p.m.

New York

Place: 188 Eastern Pkwy. (at
    Washington Ave.).
Contact: (212) 638-5000

Cathedral Church of St. John

The pipe organ is immense,
70,000 pipes—yet it fits com-
fortably in the Cathedral of St.
John the Divine, the largest
Gothic cathedral in the world.
A 90-minute tour of the
church takes you to view all
the exceptional examples of
architectural design, stained
glass windows and carved
stone. Outside, on the 13-acre
grounds, is a Biblical garden
with many of the plants men-
tioned in scripture.
Time: Mon.-Sat., 11 a.m. and 2
    p.m.; Sun., 12:30 p.m.
Place: Amsterdam Ave. and
    112th St.
Contact: (212) 678-6888

Shakespeare in the Park

Central Park is where the
notion of outdoor presentations of Shakespearean plays
took hold in this country.
There are frequent performances of many of Shakespeare's
popular plays on summer
evenings.
Time: July-Aug., Tues.-Sun., 8
    p.m.

Place: Delacourt Theater.
Contact: (212) 598-7100

Storytelling

Two dozen professional story-
tellers, including the official
storyteller for New York City
(what a job!), tell fairy tales and
other yarns to children at the
Hans Christian Andersen statue in Central Park.
Time: June-Sept., Sat., 11 a.m.
Place: At the statue.
Contact: (212) 360-8196

Jogging

Each day thousands of joggers
file down the roads and footpaths in Central Park, an activity fully encouraged by the city.
In fact, the roads are blocked
to traffic each day during the
summer. An eight-mile loop
through the park offers a striking view of the New York skyline in several spots. The park
is always open.
Time: Traffic blocked: Apr.-Nov.,
    Mon.-Fri., 10 a.m.-3 p.m. and
    7-10 p.m.; Sat.-Sun., all day
    and night. Rest of year, Sat.,-
    Sun., all day and night.
Place: Central Park.
Contact: (212) 360-8196

Conservation Center

If you have any questions a-
bout how to save energy in

your house or apartment, you
can stop by Con Edison's Conservation Center and have
your problems solved by experts. Displays and demonstrations explain how we waste
and how we can learn to save
the electricity, natural gas and
oil we use in our homes.
Time: Mon.-Sat., 10 a.m.-6:30
    p.m.
Place: 405 Lexington Ave. in the
    Chrysler Bldg.
Contact: (212) 599-3435

Energy Museum

Electrical generators and other
equipment, the likes of which
were used by Thomas Edison,
are on display in Con Edison's
Energy Museum. Exhibits explain Edison's contributions to
the production and use of electricity, and the history of
energy use and sources.
Time: Tues.-Sat., 10 a.m.-4 p.m.
Place: 145 E. 14th St.
Contact: (212) 460-6244

Coney Island

The smell of hot dogs, the
noises of the midway, screams
from people on the carnival
rides and the pounding of the
waves on the beach make
Coney Island what it is. The
park is always open. Though
there are many rides and

things to buy, there are also activities that are free. Stroll the boardwalk or body surf in the waves of the Atlantic. It's also a photographer's dream.

Time: Park: all hours. Park patrol on duty: 7 a.m.-2 a.m. Rides: noon-2 a.m.
Place: SW end of Long Island.
Contact: (212) 266-1234

Coney Island Fireworks

Big displays of fireworks are usually unleashed at Coney Island on the Fourth of July. To find out for sure, call the contact.
Contact: (212) 755-4100

Cooper-Hewitt Museum

See more than 30,000 drawings, 10,000 textiles and innumerable ceramics, wall coverings and elaborately finished pieces of furniture in the mansion that belonged to Andrew Carnegie. The 64-room, neo-Georgian structure was built in 1901.
Time: Free Tues., 5-9 p.m.
Place: Fifth Ave. at 91st St.
Contact: (212) 860-6868

Free Plays

Promising but unknown actors perform plays at the Equity Library Theater. Though a donation is asked, there is no fee. Tickets can be reserved by phone but must be picked up at least a half-hour before the performance. You stand a chance at getting a canceled ticket at the window an hour before a play begins.
Time: Tues.-Fri., 8 p.m.; Sat.-Sun., 2:30 p.m. and 8 p.m.
Place: 310 Riverside Dr.
Contact: (212) 663-2028

Flea Market

The commotion and variety make the Essex Street Flea Market seem like an entire carnival is for sale. If you don't wish to buy, you can simply watch the activity and stroll from booth to booth in an air-conditioned pavillion.
Time: Sat.-Sun., 10 a.m.-6 p.m.
Place: 140 Essex St.
Contact: (212) 673-5934

Puppet World

Puppets of all kinds present half-hour stories to children at the F. A. O. Schwarz toy store. Some of the skits are based on fairy tales and some on original stories. Inside the store, children can slide down a big

slide that connects the second and third floors.
Time: Puppet shows: Mon.-Fri., 2:30 p.m.
Place: Fifth Ave. at 58th St.
Contact: (212) 644-9400

Federal Hall

Listen to colonial folk music as you tour the 1842 customs house at the Federal Hall National Museum. The building, which stands at the site of the country's first capitol and George Washington's inaugural address, contains exhibits on the free-press trial of Peter Zenger and on the Bill of Rights.
Time: Mem. Day-Labor Day, 9 a.m.-5 p.m.; rest of year,

NEW YORK

New York

Mon.-Fri., 9 a.m.-5 p.m.
Place: 26 Wall St.
Contact: (212) 264-8711

Federal Reserve Bank

Take a 45-minute tour of the institution that is at the heart of our economy. You'll ride an elevator 85 feet below the street and look into a big vault holding millions of dollars' worth of gold bars. Give at least a week's notice (you will be mailed a free ticket to ensure your entry). No more than 30 people are allowed on each tour.
Time: Mon.-Fri., 10 and 11 a.m.; 1 and 2 p.m.
Place: 33 Liberty St.
Contact: (212) 791-6130

Fire Museum

An 1898 LaFrance engine, pulled by three horses abreast, was the mainstay of the New York City Fire Department in Brooklyn at the turn of the century. When a fire alarm sounded, the harnesses dropped from the ceiling onto the awaiting horses. This is just one of the displays you can see at the Fire Department Museum. Other exhibits include a fire-fighting sleigh that

was used in deep snow and the fireboat *Zophar Mills*. The equipment is housed in the old station for Ladder Company Number One.
Time: Sat.-Sun., 9 a.m.-2 p.m.
Place: 104 Duane St.
Contact: (212) 570-4230

Flushing Meadows

There's something for everybody in Flushing Meadows-Corona Park. You can bike, fish, ice skate, picnic or just frolic in its 1,258-acres. And on the grounds you'll find the Hall of Science, a zoo of North American animals and other attractions.
Time: Grounds: anytime. Hours of activities and buildings vary.
Place: Park bordered by Roosevelt Ave., Van Wyck Expressway, Union Turnpike and 111th St.
Contact: (212) 699-7300

Fraunces Tavern

This tavern, now a museum, was already more than 60 years old when Gen. George Washington bade farewell to the officers of the Continental Army after the revolutionary war. The building has been restored to the condition it

was in during Washington's day.
Time: Mon.-Fri., 10 a.m.-4 p.m.
Place: 54 Pearl St. (at Broad St.).
Contact: (212) 425-1778

Hotline

Here's your one-stop entertainment guide. For the latest news about free events around town, call the Free Events Hotline. A recording will give you a description, time, place and phone number (if appropriate) for happenings of the day, including films, vocal and instrumental recitals, plays and poetry readings.
Contact: (212) 755-4100

Fish Market

The early bird gets the fish at Fulton's Fish Market. The day's catch is brought in early each morning and soon disappears in a flurry of talk and waving of pocketbooks. Among the delicacies sold: octopus, eel and sardines. Great photo opportunities, and a great spectacle to boot.
Time: Mon.-Fri., 5-8 a.m.; the earlier the better.
Place: Fulton and South Sts.
Contact: (212) 344-9080

Play Rehearsals

Directed and staged play rehearsals are free at the Gene Frankel Theater. The actors

work through the parts with scripts in hand.
Time: Sat., 8 p.m.
Place: 36 W. 62nd St.
Contact: (212) 581-2775

Grand Central Terminal

Even though you're in Grand Central Terminal during the middle of the day, you can look up and see the stars: they're painted on the domed ceiling. Learn about other architectural aspects of the Renaissance-style building, its history and its future during a one-hour tour.
Time: Wed., 12:30 p.m.
Place: Chemical Bank's Commuter Express, inside the terminal.
Contact: (212) 935-3960

Summer Band Concerts

Every summer begins another season for the Guggenheim-Goldman Band concerts in Damrosch Park behind Lincoln Center. The classical, popular orchestra puts on shows of varying themes.
Time: June-Aug., Wed.-Fri., Sun., 8 p.m.
Place: 62nd St. and Amsterdam Ave.
Contact: (212) 867-8290

Guggenheim Museum

Perhaps one of the most striking aspects of the Solomon R. Guggenheim Museum is not its collection, but its building. The structure, built by Frank Lloyd Wright, encloses a huge spiral stairway that winds down to a terraced pool below. As for the collection, it's noteworthy in its own right: there are paintings and sculptures from the 19th and 20th centuries, in both permanent and changing exhibits.
Time: Free Tues., 5-8 p.m.
Place: 1071 Fifth Ave.
Contact: Recording of times and exhibits: (212) 860-1313. To ask questions on weekdays: 860-1300; on weekends: 860-1325.

Hispanic Society

The Hispanic Society of America displays Romantic paintings of El Greco and Goya, Iberian books and manuscripts, ceramics, laces and other Spanish and Portuguese art objects.
Time: Tues.-Sat., 10 a.m.-4:30 p.m.; Sun., 1-4:30 p.m.
Place: 613 W. 155th St. (at Broadway).
Contact: (212) 926-2234

Photography

Exhibits by famous and not-so-famous photographers from all over the world are shown at the International Center of Photography. It claims to be the only museum in New York devoted solely to photos. The dates of the displays range from the mid-1800s to the present; the styles range from avant-garde to photo-journalism.
Time: Free Tues., 5-8 p.m.
Place: 1130 Fifth Ave.
Contact: (212) 860-1777

Tibetan Art

Admit it: Tibetan art is not easy to find. If you've been looking the world over for some good examples, check out the Jacques Marchais Center of Tibetan Art. The collection includes bronze figures, prayer wheels, terraced gardens and Buddhist art.
Time: Apr.-Nov., Sat.-Sun., 1-5 p.m.
Place: 338 Lighthouse Ave., Staten Island.
Contact: (212) 987-3478

Outdoor Performances

During the three-week Lincoln Center Out-of-Doors festival, you can watch theater, dance and mime and listen to opera and chamber music on the plaza outside of the Center.
Time: 2nd Tues. in Aug.-Labor Day, noon-10 p.m.

New York

Place: Lincoln Center Plaza, Broadway between 62nd and 65th Sts.
Contact: (212) 877-1800

Lincoln Center

See theatrical memorabilia, scripts, manuscripts, photographs, recordings and other theater-related items in the three main galleries of the Lincoln Center Library and Museum of the Performing Arts. Hear concerts, recitals and lectures in the Bruno Walter Auditorium.
Time: Mon. and Thurs., 10 a.m.-8 p.m.; Tues., 10 a.m.-6 p.m.; Fri. and Sat., noon-6 p.m.
Place: Lincoln Center Plaza, Broadway between 62nd and 65th Sts.
Contact: (212) 930-0800

Ghost Ship

When the 282-ton cargo ship *Mary Celeste* was found adrift near the Azores on Dec. 5, 1872, only three sails were set and not a crewman was found on board. What happened to the sailors has never been explained. The exhibits of the Mary Celeste Museum describe the mystery of the ship. There also is a yard-long replica of the vessel, carved from a piece of the original wooden ship.
Time: Mon.-Fri., 9 a.m.-4 p.m.
Place: 45 Wall St.
Contact: (212) 943-1800

Metropolitan Museum of Art

This is one of the world's great museums, where masterpieces and rarities are innumerable: Rembrandts, Egyptian mummies and Chippendale furniture. The exhibits span the time from prehistory to the present and include nearly all cultures. Admission is free, though a donation is requested.
Time: Tues., 10 a.m.-8:45 p.m.; Wed.-Sat., 10 a.m.-4:45 p.m.; Sun., 11 a.m.-4:45 p.m.
Place: Fifth Ave. at 82nd St.
Contact: Recording of hours and exhibits: (212) 535-7710. For other questions: (212) 879-5500.

Morgan Library

A Gutenberg Bible, the original manuscript of *A Christmas Carol* and one of the finest collections of Rembrandt etchings are the highlights of the exhibits at the Pierpont Morgan Library. There are countless rare and old manuscripts, early books, original music manuscripts and other old publications and papers. A small donation is requested but not required.
Time: Tues.-Sat., 10:30 a.m.-5 p.m.; Sun., 1-5 p.m.
Place: 29 E. 36th St.
Contact: (212) 685-0008

Mormon Visitors Center

A diorama with talking figures describes the history and beliefs of the Mormon Church. There are free inspirational films in several languages, including English, Spanish, French, German, Chinese and Korean.
Time: 10 a.m.-8 p.m.
Place: 2 Lincoln Sq., 65th St. and Broadway.
Contact: (212) 595-1825

Broadcasting Museum

After you watch a tape of Alistair Cooke introducing the Museum of Broadcasting, you are free to study the tapes of old television shows: the Nixon-Kennedy debates, Amos 'n' Andy programs, Edward R. Murrow or Ernie Kovacs. One of the most recent additions is the US Hockey Team's gold medal win in the 1980 Winter Olympics. Though the tour is free, a donation is requested.
Time: Tues.-Sat., noon-5 p.m.
Place: 1 E. 53rd St.

Contact: Recording of times: (212) 752-7684. For personal reply: (212) 752-4690.

Museum of Modern Art

If your taste in art runs toward the recent, you might find what you're looking for at the Museum of Modern Art. The works here range from the 1880s to the present, from Cézanne to Andy Warhol. Besides paintings, there are photographs, sculptures and graphics. There are also regular showings of classic films. An admission fee is optional on Tuesdays.

Time: Tues., 11 a.m.-6 p.m.
Place: 11 W. 53rd St.
Contact: (212) 956-7070

Museum of the City

The exhibits of the Museum of the City of New York trace the city's history from its beginning as a Dutch port to its present status as the trade and culture center of the country. There are displays of old forts, model ships, photographs, fire engines and theatrical memorabilia.

Time: Tues.-Sat., 10 a.m.-5 p.m.; Sun., 1-5 p.m.
Place: Fifth Ave. and 103rd St.
Contact: (212) 534-1672

Natural History Museum

Exhibits in 35 halls and galleries portray the evolution of man, the age of the dinosaurs, the formation of the land after the formation of the earth and more. Among the exhibits are a 20-foot-tall skeleton of *Tyrannosaurus rex* and an 89-foot blue whale. There are free color movies and illustrated lectures. Donations are requested but not required.

Time: 10 a.m.-4:45 p.m. (Wed., 10 a.m.-8 p.m.).
Place: Central Park W. at 79th St.
Contact: Recording of times: (212) 873-4225; office: 873-1300.

Botanical Garden

There are 15 miles of footpaths, most of them lined with flowers, in the New York Botanical Garden. More than 12,000 different plants are on display. Films and lectures are scheduled at various times; call the contact below for more information. There is a fee for parking, but you can park outside the grounds for free.

Time: Grounds: 8 a.m.-7 p.m.
Place: On Southern Blvd. near the Bronx Zoo.
Contact: Recording of times: (212) 220-8777.

American Crafts

The collection of the Museum of American Folk Art is as rustic and simple as New York is complex and urbane. Crafted

weather vanes, homemade quilts, hand-crafted furniture, paintings and sculpture portray life as it was in mid-18th-to late 19th-century America.

Time: Free Thur., 5:30-8 p.m.
Place: 49 W. 53rd St.
Contact: (212) 581-2474

City Hall

New York City Hall, an outstanding example of federal-period architecture, houses a collection of historic portraits and antique furniture, includ-

NEW YORK

New York

ing two tables used by George Washington. You can take your own tour.

Time: Mon.-Fri., 10 a.m.-4 p.m.
Place: Near Chambers St. and Broadway in City Hall Park.
Contact: (212) 566-5700

Police Academy Museum

The New York City Police Academy Museum is supposed to hold the largest collection of police antiques in the country. There are wooden rattles that early-day cops used instead of whistles (the officers were known as the rattle watch) and more formidable weapons, including a 33-inch billy club that looks like a baseball bat.

Time: Mon.-Fri.; times vary.
Place: 235 E. 20th St.
Contact: (212) 477-9753

Free Information

For free tips about shopping, sight-seeing, off-beat tours, restaurants and other things, call the New York Convention and Visitors Bureau.

Time: 9 a.m.-6 p.m.
Contact: (212) 397-8222

Historical Society

George Washington slept here. Not in the New York Historical Society, actually, but his camp cot is here. You'll also find original Audubon paintings, wooden Indians, old carriages and fire engines and other reminders of the past.

Time: Tues.-Sat., 11 a.m.-5 p.m.; Sun., 10 a.m.-5 p.m.
Place: 170 Central Park W.
Contact: (212) 873-3400

New York Jets

Watch the training drills, pass patterns and scrimmages of the New York Jets football team as players practice at Hofstra University campus before the regular football season.

Time: Mid-July-Aug., 9:30 a.m. and 2:30 p.m.
Place: 1000 Fulton Ave., Hempstead, Long Island.
Contact: (212) 421-6600

Outdoor Opera, Orchestra

Every year the New York Philharmonic and the Metropolitan Opera perform on the grassy clearings of Central Park and parks in other boroughs. As many as 350,000 have attended the concerts at one time, sitting on the grass and drinking wine during the evening. After the Philharmonic's first concert of the season in Central Park, the sky lights up with a fireworks display.

Time: July-Aug., Tues., 8:30 p.m. (other nights in other parks).
Place: Central Park and elsewhere.
Contact: Philharmonic: (212) 877-5224; Metropolitan Opera: 799-3100.

New York Stock Exchange

In the gallery, a taped message will explain what is happening in the confusion on the floor of the New York Stock Exchange below you. From there, you can walk around, taking yourself on your own tour. There also is a film on the economy and the role of the stock exchange.

Time: Mon.-Fri., 10 a.m.-4 p.m.
Place: 20 Broad St., 3rd floor.
Contact: (212) 623-5168

Outdoor Art

The art of masters lines the streets of New York. For example, Picasso's huge sculpture, "Sylvette," stands in Greenwich Village. Bernard Rosenthal's big black cube is in Astor Place. Isamu Noguchi's large red cube stands in the Marine Midland Building. Dubuffet's "Four Trees" is in Chase Manhattan Plaza.

Contact: (212) 397-8222

Parke-Bernet Galleries

Some of the world's rarest and most expensive art objects and antiques, including paintings, furniture, jewels and rugs and carpets are auctioned off at the two Parke-Bernet galleries in New York City. Auctions, which are open to the public, are conducted during the week; the galleries are open for exhibitions during the weekends. Free lectures are sometimes scheduled.

Time: Both galleries: Mon.-Sat., 9 a.m.-5 p.m. (until 7:30 p.m. on Tues.); Sun., 1-5 p.m.
Place: 980 Madison Ave. and 1334 York Ave.
Contact: Recorded schedule: (212) 472-3555; office: 472-3400.

Prospect Park Zoo

Children can play with farm animals at the children's zoo in Prospect Park in Brooklyn. There also are the more usual zoo animals, environmental tours of the 526-acre park, free art courses and a Dutch Colonial homestead.

Time: Grounds: anytime. Zoo: 8 a.m.-4:30 p.m.
Place: On Flatbush Ave.
Contact: (212) 965-6511

Queens Botanical Garden

The folks at the Queens Botanical Garden have contrived what amounts to a giant bird feeder. They've planted trees and fruit-bearing plants to encourage the presence of a variety of birds, including blue jays, mourning doves, finches and others. Elsewhere in the 38-acre park, you can wander through a greenhouse or visit the plant propagating house.

Time: Mon.-Fri., 10 a.m.-4 p.m.; Sat.-Sun., 9 a.m.-dusk.
Place: 43-50 Main St.
Contact: (212) 886-3800

Queens Museum

If you've always had the feeling of being lost in New York, go to the Queens Museum. There you'll find a scale-model of the entire city—all the buildings represented in an area half the size of a football field. The buildings, waterfront and other areas are wired for lights, and the miniature city passes through cycles of day and night. Study this for a couple of days and you'll know where you are, where you've been and where you're going. At the museum there also are paintings, films and lectures.

Time: Tues.-Sat., 10 a.m.-5 p.m.; Sun., 1-5 p.m.

Place: New York City Bldg., Flushing Meadow-Corona Park, Queens.
Contact: (212) 592-2405

Riverside Church

Riverside Church, an interdenominational church of Gothic style, is known for the Laura Spelman Rockefeller Carillon, an arrangement of 74 bells tucked away in its 400-foot tower.

Time: Church: 9 a.m.-5 p.m. Tower: Mon.-Sat., 11 a.m.-3 p.m.; Sun., 12:30-4 p.m. Tours: Sun., 12:30 p.m.
Place: 490 Riverside Dr.
Contact: (212) 749-7000

Winery

If you have trouble imagining a winery in the heart of New York City, there's good reason. This is the only one. Schapiro's Winery buys grape juice from vineyards in upstate New York. The product is shipped to Manhattan, where Schapiro's ferments and ages it. See how a big-city winery works!

Time: Sun., 11 a.m.-4 p.m., hourly; Mon.-Fri., only large groups, by appt.
Place: 126 Rivington St.
Contact: (212) 674-4404

Seagram Building

A free 20-minute tour of the 40-story bronze-and-glass Seagram's Building takes you

NEW YORK

New York

through the lobby and to the executive floor, where you can see an antique glass collection.

Time: Tues., 3 p.m.
Place: 375 Park Ave.
Contact: (212) 572-7000

Seamen's Institute

Among the displays at the Seamen's Church Institute of New York is a 20-foot working model of a 19th-century sailing ship that was used to train officers. There also are nautical instruments, rope-work and other sailing memorabilia.

Time: Mon.-Fri., 9 a.m.-4 p.m.
Place: 15 State St.
Contact: (212) 269-2710

Songwriters

Although you won't be able to write or play songs the way Fats Waller did, you can try your hand at his piano anyway. In the Songwriters' Hall of Fame, there are instruments, photos and other memorabilia of many popular composers and singers.

Time: Mon.-Sat., 11 a.m.-3 p.m.
Place: 1 Times Square (42nd St. and Broadway).
Contact: (212) 221-1252

South Street Seaport Museum

Take a look at two restored 19th-century ships and wander through the buildings that have sat next to New York's port since the 1800s. Next to the South Street Seaport Museum, which overlooks the harbor, there is an old restored printing shop. During the summer, jazz combos play for free on the pier on Friday and Saturday evenings. All in all, a diversely interesting place.

Time: Museum: 11 a.m.-6 p.m.
   Printing shop: 11 a.m.-
   6 p.m. Pier: anytime.
Place: Fulton St. and East River, S of Brooklyn Bridge.
Contact: (212) 766-9020

Staten Island Ferry

To take the Staten Island Ferry from the tip of lower Manhattan costs 25¢. The trip back is free—but only if you stay on the boat. A round trip out to Staten Island and back takes about 45 minutes.

Time: Every 20 min.
Place: Lower tip of Manhattan.
Contact: (212) 248-8093

Staten Island Zoo

If you have a liking for poisonous snakes, you can see all 32 species of rattlesnakes that live in this country at the Staten Island Zoo. The zoo, which has a particularly large reptile collection, also has other rattlesnakes from Mexico and South America and poisonous snakes from all over the world, including cobras and mambas.

Time: Free Wed., 10 a.m.-4:45 p.m.
Place: Between Broadway and Clove Rd. on Staten Island.
Contact: Recording of times: (212) 442-3100; office: 442-3101.

Statue of Liberty

Crawl up 22 stories of stairs inside the Statue of Liberty for a free panoramic view of the New York harbor. (There is a

fee for going all the way up to the torch.) Then, you can visit the museum at the statue's base to learn the story of immigration into the United States through Ellis Island.
Time: 9 a.m.-4 p.m.
Place: Harbor at lower tip of Manhattan.
Contact: (212) 269-5755

St. Patrick's Cathedral

Twin 330-foot spires dominate the outside of the most famous of Gothic cathedrals, completed in 1874. St. Patrick's has 70 stained glass windows, 18 marble altars and seats for 2,500 worshipers. Though the church is open for public viewing most anytime, you can call ahead to make special arrangements for a guided tour.
Time: 7 a.m.-9 p.m.
Place: Fifth Ave. and 50th St.
Contact: (212) 753-2261

TV Shows

Be part of the studio audience that watches a television show as it is taped. You can see everything from game shows to soap operas. The tickets, which vary in number available from day to day, can be picked up at the New York Convention and Visitors Bureau at the address below.
Time: Mon.-Fri., 8 a.m.-4:30 p.m.
Place: 2 Columbus Cir.
Contact: (212) 397-8222

United Nations

Tickets to General Assembly meetings of the United Nations are free. Slip on a set of headphones to hear the translated words of foreign representatives. The tickets are doled out on a first-come, first-served basis.
Time: Mon.-Fri., 10:30 a.m. and 3 p.m.; meeting times may change.
Place: 46th St. and First Ave.
Contact: (212) 754-7710

Vest-Pocket Parks

Scattered around Manhattan are dozens of "vest-pocket parks," small public greens owned by corporations or donated by firms to the city. Many of the parks host special programs.
Contact: (212) 269-5755

Freebee Calendar

If you're looking for something to do in New York and don't want to spend money, flip through the "Cheap Thrills" calendar in the *Village Voice*. Each week, the calendar lists one hundred or more activities that are free or cost less than $2.50 per person.

Free Shoelaces

If you've broken a shoelace, get a new one for free at any Wallach's Clothing Store. They sew on buttons, replace collar stays, remove spots and fix zippers—all for free.
Time: During store hours.
Place: All 28 stores in New York City, Long Island, Jersey City and throughout New England.
Contact: (212) 361-7500

Downtown Museum

The downtown branch of the Whitney Museum of American Art consists entirely of changing exhibits. So don't worry if you've already been there; everything will be different when you return.
Time: Free: Tues., 5-8 p.m.
Place: 945 Madison Ave.
Contact: Recording of times: (212) 483-0011.

Whitney Museum

The three floors of the Whitney Museum of American Art—staggered like stairs to provide more interior space—hold the biggest collection of 20th-century art of any public institution. There are drawings, paintings and sculpture that are sure to fascinate any contemporary art lover.
Time: Free Tues., 5-8 p.m.
Place: 945 Madison Ave.
Contact: (212) 570-3676

NEW YORK

Niagara Falls

Honeymoon Heaven

People still come to Niagara Falls for honeymoons. Both the US and the Canadian sides of the river afford spectacular views of this famous falls. In the winter, the river forms huge ice sculptures on the face of the waterfall. Both the observation deck and geology museum are free during the winter.

Time: Free: Labor Day-Mem. Day. Observation deck: anytime. Museum: 10 a.m.-5 p.m.
Place: Prospect Park, downtown.
Contact: (716) 285-9141 or 278-8010

North Branch

Hard Cider Mill

Watch the whirling pulleys and belts of this turn-of-the-century cider press squeeze juice out of fresh apples. Some of the juice is siphoned off for the making of hard cider, a slightly alcoholic drink that tastes like apples with a touch of wine. The North Branch Cider Mill is the only licensed hard cider mill in eastern New York.

Time: Late Aug.-early Dec., 9 a.m.-5 p.m.
Place: On NY 121, in town.
Contact: (914) 482-4823

Oneonta

Four Free Museums

The four museums at Hartwick College are free and offer vastly different kinds of exhibits. The Yager Museum displays Indian artifacts from about 9000 B.C. to 1600 A.D. The Anderson Center Gallery is a museum of fine arts with changing and permanent collections of American and Renaissance art. The Hoysradt Herbarium contains some 20,000 flowering plants and ferns. The Archives has historical exhibits about Hartwick College and the surrounding area.

Time: Mon.-Fri., 10 a.m.-4 p.m. Call to confirm hours during the summer.
Place: In town near I-88.
Contact: (607) 432-4200

Oyster Bay

Arboretum

Thousands of orchids and a cactus collection are two of the main displays at Planting Fields Arboretum, a state park. A large greenhouse contains many other plants. This 400-acre site is partly wooded, partly planted in ornamentals.

Time: Labor Day-Apr., Mon.-Fri., 10 a.m.-4:30 p.m.
Place: Planting Fields Rd.
Contact: (516) 922-9200

Palmyra

Mormon Pageant

The Hill Cumorah Pageant, what Mormons call "America's Witness for Christ," is produced on a grand scale. Up to 100,000 people attend its seven performances. The cast is made up of more than 600 volunteers. The production weaves a Biblical story with religion in early America and tells the tale with recorded amplified music, lights, costumes and the big cast. Bring a blanket and warm clothes for the two-hour performance.

Time: Several evenings in late July and early Aug., about 9 p.m.
Place: 4 mi. S of town on NY 21.
Contact: (315) 597-5851

Coverlet Museum

The Alling Coverlet Museum has collected a specialized sort of Americana: woven bedspreads from the 1800s. In fact, this museum claims to have the largest collection in the country. The building is surrounded by other structures that date back to the Erie Canal era.

Time: May-Oct., 1-4 p.m.
Place: 122 Williams St.
Contact: (315) 597-6737

Rochester

Fireworks

Every year the residents of Rochester put on a grand three-day Fourth of July festival with a big display of fireworks that begins just after dark. Other activities include a parade and music by jazz, blues and rock bands. The music is free during midday.
Time: Days around July 4. Schedule of events varies.
Place: Main St. Location of fireworks varies.
Contact: (716) 428-6691

Kodak Tour

When you tour the Eastman Kodak Plant, you get a glimpse of the breadth of Kodak's products. Kodak film is only one of them—you'll also see some of the fabrics Kodak has pioneered and the Kodak copiers, which compete with those made by Rochester's other famous industry—Xerox.
Time: Mon.-Fri., 9:30 a.m. and 1:30 p.m.
Place: 200 Ridge Rd. W.
Contact: (716) 724-4000

Glass Elevator

Riding up the glass elevator at the First Federal Savings and Loan Association office is like being flown up the side of the skyscraper. The lift, on the outside of the building, rises 19 floors. Through the glass you'll be treated to a panoramic view of the river and the city of Rochester. Wonderful at night.
Time: Mon.-Fri., 8:30 a.m.-10:30 p.m.; Sat., 5:30 p.m.-midnight; Sun., 11 a.m.-2:30 a.m.
Place: Main and State Sts.
Contact: (716) 454-4010

Charlotte Lighthouse

The Charlotte Lighthouse, built in 1822, is placed where the Genessee River spills into Lake Ontario. The structure was retired at the turn of the century but still is the home of the area Coast Guard chief. Because the spiral stairway that leads to the top is without railings or lights, public tours are no longer offered. But during Rediscover the River Day, usually held two days of the year, you can tour the grounds and hear an explanation of the lighthouse's history.
Time: Usually June and Oct., afternoons.
Place: 70 Lighthouse St.
Contact: (716) 342-4140

Bagels, Bagels

All kinds of bagels are made at the Bagel Shop of Irondequoit, and you can see how it's done. An added bonus is a free bagel.

You may want to bring your own cream cheese and lox! Make reservations.
Time: Mon.-Fri., 9, 9:30 and 10 a.m.
Place: 525 Titus Ave.
Contact: (716) 266-0690

Seneca

Free Fall

When the weather is good, you can watch members of the Seneca Sport Parachute Club jump from airplanes and drift gently to earth.
Time: Summer weekends. No set schedule.
Place: Seneca Falls Airport.
Contact: Club: (315) 568-9849. Airport: 568-9897.

NEW YORK

South Otselic

Fishing Museum

Fishing rods, reels, lures and other equipment—some of it more than a couple of hundred years old—are on display at the Gladding International Sport Fishing Museum. Of special interest is the exhibit showing one of the first books of fishing—*Fysshe and Fysshynge*, written in 1496 by a nun named Sister Juliana Berners.
Time: Mem. Day-Labor Day, Tues.-Sun., 10 a.m.-5 p.m.
Place: Maple Ave.
Contact: (315) 653-7211

Staatsburg

Mills Mansion

The country estate of Ogden Mills, a 65-room mansion built in 1895, is now preserved in Mills Mansion State Historic Site. The house, surrounded by a 575-acre yard, has marble fireplaces, wood paneling and finely finished furniture.
Time: May-Oct., 9 a.m.-4:30 p.m.
Place: NY 9 and Old Post Rd.
Contact: (914) 889-4100

Uniondale

New York Islanders

Watch the members of the New York Islanders hone the skills, grace, speed and dirty tricks it takes to make a professional hockey team. Call the main office for the times and locations of practices, which are free to the public.
Time: Sept.-May.
Contact: (516) 794-4100

Utica

Free Beer

After your tour of the West End Brewing Co., you'll be whisked away on a trolley and taken to a restored tavern of the 1800s, where you have your choice of two beers or two root beers. West End Brewing makes Utica Club and Matts Premium, a cream ale and a doubly potent beer.
Time: June-Aug., Mon.-Fri., 10 a.m.-5 p.m.
Place: Court and Varick Sts.
Contact: (315) 732-3181

Vestal Center

Star Watch

Look for free at the stars and planets through the Kopernik Observatory telescope. An added attraction is a one-hour lecture on astronomy and on what you can expect to see during the viewing session. Kopernik is the largest public observatory in New York State.
Time: Mar.-Dec., Fri., 8-11 p.m.
Place: 1.5 mi. S of town on NY 26, then .3 mi. W on Glenwood Rd., then 2 mi. S on Underwood Rd.
Contact: Observatory: (607) 748-3685; Roberson Center: 772-0660.

Washingtonville

Free Wine

The tour of the famous Brotherhood Winery both begins and ends with a nice touch. Before the tour starts, you taste two samples of wine. The tour's completion brings you to the wine-tasting room, where many more samples await you. During the Christmas season, you can attend special holiday wine-tasting parties.
Time: Feb.-Mar., Sat.-Sun., 10 a.m.-4 p.m. Apr.-June, Mon.-Fri., noon-3 p.m.; Sat.-Sun., 10 a.m.-4 p.m. July-Aug., Mon.-Sun., 10 a.m.-4 p.m. Sept.-Dec., hours vary, so call ahead.
Place: 35 North St.
Contact: (914) 496-9101

Youngstown

Our Lady of Fatima Shrine

More than 100 life-size or larger-than-life statues surround the Dome Basilica at Our Lady of Fatima Shrine.

The most notable is the statue of Our Lady of the Rosary of Fatima, a 13-foot figure carved from granite. Take a self-guided tour of the basilica and the 15-acre grounds.

Time: May-Sept., 8 a.m.-8 p.m.; rest of the year, 9 a.m.-5 p.m.
Place: Swan Rd., .5 mi. E of NY 18.
Contact: (716) 754-7489

PENNSYLVANIA

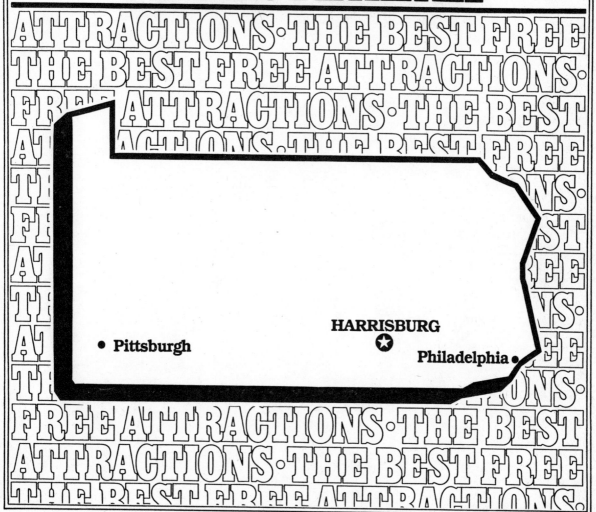

ATTRACTIONS·THE BEST FREE THE BEST FREE ATTRACTIONS· FREE ATTRACTIONS·THE BEST

HARRISBURG ⭐

• Pittsburgh

Philadelphia •

FREE ATTRACTIONS·THE BEST ATTRACTIONS·THE BEST FREE

PENNSYLVANIA

Allentown

European Masterpieces

The Allentown Art Museum features rotating exhibits varying in interest and quality. But it is best known for its fine collection of European works from the 14th to the 18th centuries.

Time: Tues.-Sat., 10 a.m.-5 p.m.; Sun., 1-5 p.m.
Place: Fifth and Court Sts.
Contact: (215) 432-4333

Altoona

Engineering Marvel

Horseshoe Curve, a remarkable engineering feat, has become world-famous for its unusual design: it carries Penn Central trains around a 1/2-mile curve and up incredibly steep grades.

Place: 5 mi. W of town (well-marked from Altoona).

Audubon

Audubon's Home

Mill Grove, the authentic Audubon home, rests in a sylvan setting of woods and gently sloping hills. The origi-nal house, converted into a museum, contains an attic restored to a studio and taxidermy room, similar to the working quarters used by the superb wildlife artist. On six miles of trails you have a chance to see 400 species of flowering plants and some of the 175 species of birds sighted in the area since 1951.

Time: Tues.-Sun., 10 a.m.-5 p.m.
Place: 2 mi. NW via PA 363 from Valley Forge State Park.
Contact: (215) 666-5593

Bushkill

Delaware Water Gap

One of the great scenic areas in the state, the gorge stretches 35 miles along US 209 from Matamoras to Kittatinny Point (site of the Delaware Water Gap). You'll see lush fields and several beautiful falls along the route.

Carlisle

Redskins' Camp

Catch a glimpse of the pros in action. The Washington Redskins train here before the regular season. Check before

going, since admission policy varies by year and by coach.

Time: Mid-July-Aug.
Place: Dickinson College campus.
Contact: (717) 243-4515, 245-1120 or 243-5121.

Chadds Ford

Washington's Headquarters

Two historic buildings (headquarters for Washington and for the Marquis de LaFayette) have been rebuilt or preserved in part at the Brandywine Battlefield State Park. Here you can see a 20-minute slide presentation outlining the battle.

Time: Park: May-Sept., Tues.-Sat., 10 a.m.-8 p.m.; Sun., noon-8 p.m. Rest of year to 4:30 p.m. Historic sites: Jan.-Feb., Sat., 10 a.m.-4:30 p.m.; Sun., noon-4:30 p.m.
Place: 1 mi. N of town on US 1.
Contact: (215) 459-3342

Columbia

Free Wine Tasting

Nissley Vineyards offers one of the state's finest winery tours, naturally with a chance to sample wines for free. You'll find it in an exceptionally scenic part of Pennsylvania, with its rolling hills and neatly tended farms. Worth a detour for oenophiles. Tours last approximately 30 minutes.
Time: Mon.-Sat., noon-6 p.m. by appt.
Place: 8 mi. N. of town off PA 441.
Contact: (717) 426-3514

Cresson

Railroad History

The Allegheny Portage Railroad National Historic Site offers a 12-minute slide show that depicts the history of the Portage railroad. Traces of the line have been preserved at the site.
Time: June 15-Labor Day, 8:30 a.m.-7 p.m.; rest of year, 8:30

a.m.-5 p.m.
Place: 2.5 mi. E of town on US 22.
Contact: (814) 886-8176

Delta

Atomic Power

The Peach Bottom Atomic Information Center near the Susquehanna River presents free film and slide shows on atomic energy. Popular too are the slide-tape show explaining the atom and a scale model of a nuclear plant.
Time: Wed.-Sun., 10 a.m.-4 p.m.
Place: 3 mi. E of town.
Contact: (717) 456-5101

Elverson

Pig Iron

Hopewell Village National Historic Site brings to life 18th and 19th century smelting operations. You'll see actual furnaces and learn about the background with an audio-visual presentation. During the summer a living history program includes blacksmithing, candle making and similar activities.
Time: 9 a.m.-5 p.m.
Place: 8 mi. N of town, off PA 345.
Contact: (215) 582-8773

Farmington

Battlefield Encampment

Throughout the year there's a 15-minute slide program at the Fort Necessity National Battlefield, explaining the history of the site. But the great moment comes on the weekend nearest July 4th when 75 soldiers dress in French, British and American uniforms to portray a typical camp during the French and Indian War.
Time: May-Sept., 9 a.m.-6 p.m.; rest of year, 8 a.m.-5 p.m.
Place: .5 mi. W on PA 40.
Contact: (412) 329-5512

Franklin Center

Limited Editions

The Franklin Mint and Museum is the world's largest private mint and producer of limited editions. Many of them are on display in the adjacent museum which offers free entry and 45-minute tours of the mint. Tours begin with a 13-minute film explaining what you're about to see.
Time: Museum: Mon.-Fri., 9 a.m.-5 p.m. Tours: Mon.-Fri., 10 and 11 a.m. and 1, 2 p.m. Please call ahead.
Place: 1 mi. S of PA 452 on US 1.
Contact: (215) 459-6168

PENNSYLVANIA

Gettysburg

Scenic Valley Tour

The Scenic Valley Tour runs for 36 miles through some of the state's most striking scenery. Take the tour with a free map and brochure, available from the contact.
Contact: Gettysburg Travel Council, 35 Carlisle St., Gettysburg, PA 17325; (717) 334-6274.
Note: The entire route is marked with Scenic Valley tour signs.

Mock Battles

Some years the cannons roar in a re-creation of the Battle of Gettysburg. Every year there's an encampment, reenactments of skirmishes, artillery demonstrations and drills. Concerts typical of the era top off the festivities.
Time: Dates vary.
Place: Gettysburg Travel Council, 35 Carlisle St., Gettysburg, PA 17325.
Contact: (717) 334-6274.

Walking Tour

Contact the Gettysburg Travel Council for a free brochure outlining a Downtown Gettysburg Walking Tour.
Contact: Gettysburg Travel Council, 35 Carlisle St., Gettysburg, PA 17325; (717) 334-6274.

Robert E. Lee Headquarters

The Gettysburg headquarters of Robert E. Lee, a picturesque stone house built in the 1700s, now serves as a museum with exhibits on the great battle.
Time: Mid-Mar.-Oct., 9 a.m.-9 p.m.
Place: 401 Buford Ave.
Contact: (717) 334-3141

National Shrine

Gettysburg National Military Park, scene of the most decisive battle in the Civil War and immortalized in the Gettysburg Address, is an important place to visit. Stop by the Cyclorama for a 30-minute presentation on the battle which includes a ten-minute film that makes a tour of the area more meaningful. Check to see whether free campfire programs are still being held in the amphitheater in Pitzer Woods, at 8:45 p.m. from late June through Labor Day.
Time: Campfires: 8:45 p.m. (but call to confirm).
Place: Gettysburg National Military Park, Gettysburg, PA 17325.
Contact: (717) 334-1124

Hanover

Horse Breeding

No formal tours are offered at Hanover Shoe Farms, the world's leading and largest breeder of standardbred horses. But visitors are welcome to walk through the four barns in the front area and admire the pacers.
Time: 8 a.m.-3:30 p.m.
Place: On PA 194.
Contact: (717) 637-8931

Harrisburg

Planetarium Shows

In the William Penn Memorial Museum and Archives building, free planetarium shows are given to the public on weekends only — first come, first seated!
Time: Sat.-Sun., 1:30 and 3 p.m.
Place: 700 N. Third St.
Contact: (717) 787-4978

State Capitol

Beneath the 26,000-ton St. Peter-like dome, you'll be guided through a building with 650 rooms — what amounts to a full two acres. Average tours last 30 minutes.
Time: Mon.-Fri., 9 a.m.-4:30 p.m.
Place: Third and State Sts.
Contact: (717) 787-6810

Period Rooms

Lovely period rooms and a giant mural depicting Pennsylvania history highlight the William Penn Memorial Museum and Archives.

Time: Mem. Day-Labor Day, Tues.-Sat., 9 a.m.-5 p.m.; Sun., noon-5 p.m. Rest of year, Tues.-Sat., 10 a.m.-4:30 p.m.; Sun., noon-4:30 p.m.
Place: 700 N. Third St.
Contact: (717) 787-4978

Hershey

Chocolate World

Even the street lamps are shaped like chocolate kisses in the town noted for the world's largest chocolate factory. Ride on automated cars through a world of chocolate, from cocoa plantations to a manufacturing plant.

Time: Mon.-Sat., 9 a.m.-4:45 p.m.; Sun., noon-4:45 p.m. Call for summer hours, which vary.
Place: Park Blvd.
Contact: (717) 534-4900

Lancaster

Bavarian Twists

At Anderson Pretzel Bakery you'll see a Bavarian twisting machine turning out one of America's favorite snacks — and you'll get free samples as a salty sendoff.

Time: Mon.-Fri., 8:30 a.m.-4 p.m.
Place: 2060 Old Philadelphia Pike.
Contact: (717) 299-2321

Lebanon

Smoked Meats

Take a 30-minute tour of Weaver's to see how their wood-smoked meats are processed and hung by hand, as they have been for nearly a century.

Time: Mon.-Fri., 9 a.m.-4 p.m.
Place: 15th Ave. and Weavertown Rd.
Contact: (717) 272-5643

Philadelphia

Don't Keep the Change

The US Mint of Philadelphia produces coins from silver before your eyes — behind glass, of course. Push-button recordings explain the stages of production. Sorry, no souvenirs.

Time: Mon.-Fri., 8:30 a.m.-3:30 p.m.
Place: Fifth and Arch Sts.
Contact: (215) 597-7350

First Flag

Controversial as it may be, Betsy Ross is still credited with making the first United States flag. Her restored 2-½ storey colonial home is open year-round. Inside is an upholsterer's shop typical of the one Betsy would have used in the 1770s.

Time: Apr.-Oct., 9 a.m.-6 p.m.; rest of year, 9 a.m.-5 p.m.
Place: 239 Arch St.
Contact: (215) 627-5343

One of the Finest

The Philadelphia Museum of Art, one of the finest in the country, has an outstanding and varied collection of over 500,000 pieces. They vary from priceless paintings to antique

PENNSYLVANIA

Philadelphia

armor and you can view them free on Sundays.
Time: Free on Sun., 10 a.m.-1 p.m.
Place: 26th and Parkway.
Contact: (215) 763-8100

Historic Square Mile

All of the attractions are free in what has been called "America's most historic square mile," now known as Independence National Historic Park. Here you'll find Independence Square, a glass pavilion housing the Liberty Bell, and Independence Hall. Pick up a free brochure and watch a 30-minute film at the visitor center to appreciate the area more fully.
Time: 9 a.m.-5 p.m.
Place: 143 S. Third St.
Contact: (215) 597-7120

Eight-Hour Spectacle

For eight hours on New Year's Day, the Mummers Parade moves along Broad Street. You can see literally thousands of Mummers — 22,000 to be exact — all in fanciful dress. This rivals the Mardi Gras in its freewheeling revelry!
Time: New Year's Day.
Place: Broad St.
Contact: (215) 864-1976

Thanksgiving Day Parade

An institution and an extravaganza, the Gimbel's Thanksgiving Day parade features dozens of bands and 5,000 marchers, including national celebrities.
Time: 3rd Thurs. in Nov.
Contact: (215) 864-1976

Free Tours

Free tours of historic areas are given during Freedom Week. There's also live entertainment on the Benjamin Franklin Parkway and at Penn's Landing daily.
Time: Late June-early July.
Contact: (215) 864-1976

20,000 Works of Art

Thousands of works of art are for sale during the Rittenhouse Square Art Annual. The open-air gallery draws amateurs and highly-paid professionals alike, and is one of the great events in the city!
Time: June.
Place: Rittenhouse.
Contact: (215) 864-1976

Pathological Specimens

For those with a bent toward the medical or morbid, the Mütter Museum is just what the doctor ordered. An unusual and extensive collection of thousands of pathological specimens!
Time: Tues.-Fri., 10 a.m.-4 p.m.
Place: 19 S. 22nd St.
Contact: (215) 561-6050

Pittsburgh

One of the Best

Only superlatives can do justice to the Carnegie Museum of Natural History. Full-scale dinosaurs, a mineral room that may well be the best in the US, and dozens of other exhibits make this a fascinating stop. Note that it's free on Saturday only. On all other days, entry is by suggested donation.
Time: Free on Sat., 10 a.m.-5 p.m.
Place: 4400 Forbes Ave.
Contact: (412) 622-3270

Rubens

The Frick Art museum, in an Italian Renaissance-style building, has a small, very fine collection including works representing the Italian Renaissance. Not well-known but superb are its gold-leafed panels from the 14th century. Paintings include works by masters such as Rubens and Tintoretto.
Time: Fri.-Sat., 10 a.m.-5:30 p.m.; Sun., noon-6 p.m.
Place: 7227 Reynolds St.
Contact: (412) 371-7766

Talking Mynah Bird

This conservatory-aviary is a warm, wonderful place. The birds inhabit free-flight areas,

so it is *you* who walk along caged paths. Peacocks and a talking mynah bird delight people of all ages! The number of birds is increasing under new management and you can see them all at no charge on Saturdays.

Time: Free Sat., 9 a.m.-4:30 p.m.
Place: Allegheny Commons West.
Contact: (412) 322-7855

Giant Telescope

At the Allegheny Observatory you can peer through a 13-inch telescope and listen to the experts tell you about the celestial bodies you're viewing. Tours last 90 minutes and include a slide show. Please call ahead to reserve a place.

Time: Apr.-Oct., Tues.-Fri., 8 p.m. Please call ahead.
Place: Dept. of Astronomy, University of Pittsburgh, 159 Riverview Are.
Contact: (412) 321-2400.
Note: No one under 10 admitted.

Nationality Rooms

The 19 Nationality Rooms of the Cathedral of Learning at the University of Pittsburgh are the campus' main attraction. Free descriptive brochures on the rooms are available at the visitor center, which also offers free campus tours while school is in session.

Time: Free from Sept.-Nov. and Jan.-Apr., Mon.-Fri., 9 a.m.-5 p.m. Rest of year: small admission charge.
Place: 1st floor of Cathedral of Learning, on Bigelow St.
Contact: (412) 624-6000

Free Times at the Zoo

The Pittsburgh Zoo is home for 2,000 animals (350 species) including the always popular penguins and bears. The zoo's unique offerings include freshwater dolphins and manatee. The aquarium, with many tanks, including one 80,000-gallon monster, is simply superb. Note that there is a dollar parking charge at the zoo grounds.

Time: Free Mon.-Fri., 9-11 a.m.
Place: Highland Park.
Contact: (412) 441-6262

Bird's Eye View

Soar to the top of the city's tallest structure for a marvelous view from Top of the Triangle Restaurant. The place graciously opens its doors for an hour each morning, just to let you delight at the view.

Time: Mon.-Fri., 9-10 a.m.
Place: US Steel Bldg.
Contact: (412) 471-4100

Valley Forge

Patriotic Pep Talk

At the Freedoms Foundation you'll get a patriotic pep talk which includes rags-to-riches success stories, information on all Congressional Medal of Honor winners, and displays on the American credo. Lowell Thomas narrates a slide show telling about the foundation's beliefs and purposes.

Time: May-Labor Day, Mon.-Sat., 10 a.m.-4 p.m.; Sun., noon-4 p.m. Rest of year, Mon.-Fri., 10 a.m.-4 p.m.

PENNSYLVANIA

Valley Forge

Place: On PA 23 (.25 mi. W of Valley Forge National Park).
Contact: (215) 933-8825

National Historic Park

Watch a 15-minute slide show in the visitor center before walking through the park and visiting Washington's Headquarters. There you'll find guides in period dress ready to give you the history of this nationally significant site.
Time: Late June-Labor Day, 8:30 a.m.-6 p.m.; rest of year, 8:30 a.m.-5 p.m.
Place: Take Exit 24 off PA Turnpike.
Contact: (215) 783-7700

Washington

Covered Bridge Festival

Pennsylvania has more covered bridges than any state — 350 in all. Their rustic charm is celebrated at the Fall Festival in Washington, an appropriate place since 35 bridges are within easy driving distance.
Time: 3rd weekend in Sept.
Contact: Washington-Green

County Tourist Assn., Box 877, Washington, PA 15301; (412) 222-8130.

West Grove

600 Acres of Roses

The Conard-Pyle Company was begun in the late 1800s and is unique today as the East's largest grower of roses, 600 acres in all. The nursery has won numerous All-American Rose Selections Awards. If you make an appointment, you can stroll among its blue-ribbon bushes.
Time: Mon.-Fri., by appt.
Place: Rosehill Rd., W of town on US 1.
Contact: (215) 869-8011.

York

Pumping Iron

At the Bob Hoffman Weight Lifting and Softball Hall of Fame, you can see a free 30-minute film and displays related to these sports.
Time: Mon.-Fri., 8 a.m.-5 p.m.
Place: I-83, exit 11.
Contact: (717) 764-5947

Statewide

Free Camping

Although there's a charge for camping in state parks, you'll find free sites in the state forests. These tend to be more isolated and primitive, qualities which appeal to many hikers and backpackers anyway.
Contact: Dept. of Environmental Resources, Bureau of Forestry, P.O. Box 1467, Harrisburg, PA 17120; (717) 787-2014.

Free Parks

The 120 state parks have no entry fee, which makes them one of Pennsylvania's prime attractions. Call or write the contact below for information on this varied, fine park system.
Contact: Bureau of State Parks, Fulton Bldg., P.O. Box 2063, Harrisburg, PA 17120; (717) 787-8800.

RHODE ISLAND

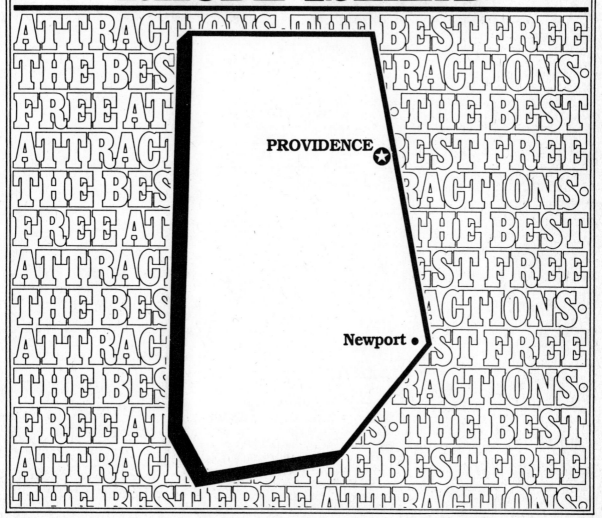

PROVIDENCE

Newport

RHODE ISLAND

Adamsville

Chicken Shrine

The Rhode Island Red Monument is the world's only shrine to a chicken—the fowl which happens to be the state bird. Tourists cluck with joy when taking photos of their families here.

Place: Corner of Main St. and W. Port Harbor Rd.
Contact: (401) 635-4400

Block Island

200-Foot Cliffs

Although there's a charge to get to Block Island by ferry, the area offers many free memorable experiences. Be sure not to miss the southeastern corner! The 200-foot high clay cliffs known as Mohegan Bluffs provide a fabulous view, and the lighthouse is a postcard picture! During the first weekend in October bird lovers congregate on the island, which attracts thousands of birds at that time.

Kenyon

Canoe Route

Canoe through the Great Swamp near Kenyon. It's a 2,600-acre morass, practically untouched by man. It's also the sight of an Indian memorial service in the fall.

Time: Swamp: sunrise to sunset. Memorial: last Sun. in Sept., 2 p.m.
Contact: (401) 539-7795

Little Compton

Wine Tasting

Salconnet Vineyards, a relative newcomer to the wine business, offers free tours and wine tasting during the summer months. Tours last about an hour, and you'll be invited to sample three or four wines.

Time: Mem. Day-Oct.
Place: W. Main Rd.
Contact: (401) 635-4356

Middletown

Tour a Destroyer

Destroyers in the Newport Harbor Naval Education and Training Center are open on a rotating basis on summer weekends. You'll see the galley and guns which give these ships their formidable reputation.

Time: Mid-May-Labor Day, Sat.-Sun., 1-4 p.m.
Place: In town, on Aquidnick Island, .25 mi. N on W. Main St.
Contact: (401) 841-4654

Newport

Nation's Oldest Tavern

British soldiers slept in the White Horse Tavern, which was built before 1673. A classic clapboard tavern with gambrel roof, it still serves meals from 4:30 to 7:30 p.m. if you care to buy a dinner.

Place: Corner of Marlborough and Farewell Sts.
Contact: (401) 849-3600

Military Revues

Approximately 400 candidates in naval officer candidate school pass in revue on Friday afternoons. The full-dress

parade and accompanying drills can be magnificent.
Time: Fri., 3:30 p.m.
Place: Enter naval base at gate 4 off Coddington Hwy.
Contact: (401) 841-3538

Changing Exhibits

Call ahead to find out what's showing at the Art Association of Newport, located in a home dating back to 1862.
Time: Tues.-Sat., 10 a.m.-5 p.m.; Sun., 2-5 p.m.
Place: 76 Bellevue Ave.
Contact: (401) 847-0179

Military Uniforms

The Artillery Company Armory and Museum features uniforms and military artifacts from over 100 foreign countries and is housed in a building dating back to 1835.
Time: May 4-Sept., Tues.-Sat., 11:30 a.m.-4:30 p.m.; rest of year, Sat., 1-4 p.m.
Place: 23 Clarke St.
Contact: (401) 846-2552

18th-Century Wharf Area

Stop off at Bannister and Bowen's Wharf, an 18th-century area now noted for delightful shops and workshops. Great photo prospects and possibilities!
Place: Between Mill and Pelham Sts.
Contact: (401) 846-4500

Colonial Collection

Here you'll find the oldest meeting house in the country, dating back to 1729, and a museum noted for its varied collection from Colonial times including ship models, costumes, silver and furniture.
Time: June-Aug., Tues.-Fri., 9:30 a.m.-4:30 p.m.; Sat., 9:30 a.m.-noon; Sun., 1-5 p.m. Rest of year, closed Sun.
Place: 82 Touro St.
Contact: (401) 846-0813

Ancient Mill

Some believe the Old Stone Mill in Newport was built by Norsemen centuries before Columbus sailed to America. More likely it dates from the 17th century. Take a look at the circular stone tower in Touro Park.

Early American Paintings

Redwood Library and Athenaeum is said to be the oldest library in continuous use in the US. Of particular interest is its fine collection of early American paintings.
Time: Sept.-July, Mon.-Sat., 10 a.m.-6 p.m.; Aug., Mon.-Sat., 10 a.m.-5 p.m.
Place: 50 Bellevue Ave.
Contact: (401) 847-0292

Naval Museum

A visit to the Naval Museum with its military history displays can be combined with a revue of the candidates or a tour of a Navy destroyer (see separate entries under Middleton and Newport).
Time: Mid-May-Labor Day, Mon.-Fri., 9 a.m.-4 p.m.; Sat.-Sun., noon-4 p.m.
Place: Gate 1 along Admiral Kaldfus Rd.
Contact: (401) 841-4052

Trinity Church

Handel himself tested the organ before it was sent to Trinity Church (1726), which some say is "the finest timbered structure in America." Washington worshipped in pew 81.
Time: June-Sept., Mon.-Sat., 10 a.m.-4 p.m.; rest of year, by appt.
Place: Queen Anne Sq.
Contact: (401) 846-0660

Providence

Waterford Chandelier

The First Baptist Meeting House (1775) has been beautifully preserved and boasts a breathtaking Waterford chandelier from 1792. Tours are

RHODE ISLAND

Providence

offered after the 11 a.m. Sunday service.

Time: Apr.-Oct., Mon.-Fri., 10 a.m.-3 p.m.; Sat., 10 a.m.-noon; rest of year, by appt.
Place: 75 N. Main St., at Waterman St.
Contact: (401) 421-1177

State Capitol

During a tour of the State Capitol you'll see a replica of the Liberty Bell, a portrait gallery and a 24-carat gold governor's reception chamber. Tours last about one hour.

Time: Mon.-Fri., 9 a.m.-3:30 p.m.
Place: Smith St.
Contact: (401) 277-2311

Athenaeum

The Providence Athenaeum features an extensive 19th-century research library with "elephant folios" (oversize first editions) of Audubon engravings and illustrations of Napoleon's Egyptian expedition. Artworks include a Reynolds original and a Malbone ivory miniature.

Time: Mid-June-mid-Sept., Mon.-Fri., 8:30 a.m.-5:30 p.m. Rest of year, Mon.-Fri., 8:30 a.m.-5:30 p.m.; Sat., 9:30 a.m.-5:30 p.m.
Place: 251 Benefit St.
Contact: (401) 421-6970

Art Collection

At the Rhode Island School of Design's Museum of Art you'll find a varied collection from antiquities to abstracts. This noted museum is well worth a visit.

Time: Free: Thurs., 7-9 p.m.; Sat., 10:30 a.m.-5 p.m.
Place: 224 Benefit St., at Rhode Island School of Design.
Contact: (401) 331-3511

Free Music

The Parks and Recreation Board sponsors free musical events year-round in Roger Williams Park. Programs are presented both in the Museum Auditorium (winter) and Temple to Music (summer).

Time: May-Sept., Sun., 2 p.m.; rest of year, Sun., 8 p.m.
Contact: (401) 421-3300

Paul Revere Bell

The bell in the tower of the First Unitarian Church of Providence is the largest Paul Revere original, circa 1816. While catching your breath from the climb, enjoy a view of Brown University, downtown Providence, the Providence River and the port.

Time: Mon.-Fri., 9 a.m.-5 p.m.; Sat., 9 a.m.-noon.
Place: Benevolent and Benefit Sts.
Contact: (401) 421-7970

Through a Bubble

At Roger Williams Park you can enter a bubble and be eye-to-eye with prairie dogs. The

polar bears, seals and hoofed animals are also very popular. Throughout the park scenic trails lead past lakes and beds of flowers. Also of interest are a natural history museum, tropical greenhouses and an aviary. Ask about the occasional concerts.

Time: 7-9 p.m.
Place: Elmwood Ave., exit off I-95.
Contact: (401) 421-3300

18th-Century Garden

The Governor Stephen Hopkins House, named after one of

the signers of the Declaration of Independence, was built in 1707. Period furnishings and an 18th-century garden add to its charm.

Time: Apr.-Dec., Wed.-Sat., 1-4 p.m., by appt.
Place: Benefit and Hopkins Sts.
Contact: (401) 831-7440

Bolt Splitter

The College Hill area features several "Lightning Splitter" houses, built with steeply slanting roofs designed to split lightning bolts and thus protect the houses. So far it's worked! The one at 53 Transit Street was built in 1781 and remodeled in 1850. Write the contact for a brochure, "Benefit St.—A Mile of History," and take a walking tour of the area.

Contact: The Providence Preservation Society, 24 Meeting St., Providence, RI 02903; (401) 831-7440.

South Kingston

Primitive Cultures

The Museum of Primitive Culture exhibits everything from bizarre masks to weapons and tools from throughout the world.

Time: Mon.-Fri., 10 a.m.-noon, and by appt.

Place: 804 Kingston Rd.
Contact: (401) 783-5711

Touro

Architectural Gem

Built in 1763, the Touro Synagogue is the oldest in America. Don't be deceived by the plain brick exterior—you must get inside to understand why so many consider it a masterpiece.

Time: Sun., 2-4 p.m.
Place: 72 Touro St.
Contact: (401) 847-4794

Usquepaugh

Kenyon Corn Meal Company

Since 1886, a grist mill has stone-ground meals and mixes here. (Stone-grinding is said to waste fewer nutrients than other methods.) Now the site of Kenyon Corn Meal Company, the mill continues. Tour the premises, and finish with complimentary recipe books.

Time: July-Aug., Mon.-Thurs., 1-4 p.m.; rest of year, Sat.-Sun., noon-5 p.m.
Place: On RI 138.
Contact: (401) 783-4054

Watch Hill

Oldest Merry-Go-Round

This is the nation's oldest merry-go-round—its music has played and horses flown for 100 years of continuous operation. It was once run by *real* horsepower—two horses, to be exact!

Time: Mem. Day-Labor Day.
Place: On the beach at Bay St.
Contact: (401) 596-7761
Note: There is a nominal charge to ride the merry-go-round, but watching is free.

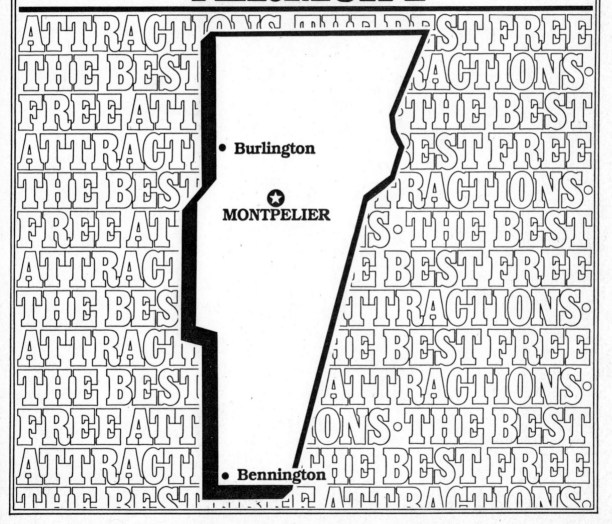

VERMONT

VERMONT

Barre

Granite Quarry

Rock of Ages Quarry has been supplying marble for gravestones since the Civil War. You can watch blasting, cutting and polishing on a typical tour of this 27-acre hillside hole, which amounts to the world's largest granite quarry. Free postcards and bits of granite are given out to visitors.

Time: Tours: May-Oct., Mon.-Fri., 8:30 a.m.-5 p.m. Factory: May-Oct., Mon.-Fri., 8:30 a.m.-3:30 p.m.
Place: 2.5 mi. S on VT 14, then 2.5 mi. on local road, following signs.
Contact: (802) 476-3115

Bennington

Dairy Farm

Fairdale Farms is an operating dairy farm and offers one-hour tours that include visits to the calf nursery, a real delight for kids. Calves are kept here until they are six months old. There is also a carousel milking parlor, where cows step in one at a time to be milked. The tour ends with a look at the milk processing plant.

Time: May-mid-Oct., Mon.-Sat., 10 a.m.-9 p.m.
Place: 2 mi. W of town on VT 9.
Contact: (802) 442-6391

The Long Trail

Hikers can follow the 265-mile Long Trail over the Green Mountains to the Canadian border. The trails leading to the top of Mt. Mansfield and Camel's Hump are particularly popular on this well-traveled route. For more information write or call the Green Mountain Club.

Contact: Green Mountain Club, P.O. Box 889, 43 State St., Montpelier, VT 05602; (802) 223-3463.

Brookfield

Floating Bridge

An oddity, this 320-foot floating bridge is part of the state highway system. It was first constructed in 1819 as a passage across Sunset Lake and has been reconstructed several times. Closed in the winter.

Time: Open when the lake is not frozen.
Place: Brookfield State Hwy.
Contact: (802) 276-3352

Burlington

American Prints

At the Robert Hull Fleming Museum you'll find everything from African and Native American exhibits to a superb modern art collection, full of 20th-century American prints and drawings.

Time: Mon.-Fri., 9 a.m.-5 p.m.; Sat.-Sun., 1-5 p.m.
Place: 61 Colchester Ave., University of Vermont campus.
Contact: (802) 656-2090

Cabot

Butter and Cheese Plant

Cabot Farmers' Cooperative Creamery, the largest butter and cheese plant in New England, makes an interesting tour. Through picture windows you can see huge vats holding 31,000 pounds of milk and 5,000-pound globs of butter. A storage area holds the thousands of gallons of milk needed to produce five million pounds of cheese each year.

Time: Apr.-Dec., Mon.-Fri., 8 a.m.-4:30 p.m.; Fri.-Sat., 9 a.m.-3 p.m. Rest of year, Mon.-Fri., 8 a.m.-4:30 p.m.
Place: 5 mi. S of Walden off VT 15, on Main St.
Contact: (802) 563-2231

Danville

Learn to Divine

Every September hundreds of dowsers gather in Danville to go out on dowsing field trips. Since the area has abundant

underground water, it's ideal for dowsing with sticks, pendulums, rods and even bare hands. Dowsers claim that the art can be learned by anyone with an open mind! There are fees to enter the dowsing convention and formal school, but impromptu, free instruction and several demonstrations on the Village Green occur frequently.

Time: 3rd week in Sept.; call contact for exact dates.
Place: 7 mi. W of St. Johnsbury on US 2, on the Village Green and throughout the town of Danville.
Contact: (802) 684-3417

East Hubbardton

Battle Site

In the visitor center you can listen to a brief tape and view a brightly lit state map which gives background on the Hubbardton Battle, the only one fought on Vermont soil during the Revolution. Learn more about the hardy Vermont soldiers who participated in this important battle.

Time: Late May-mid-Oct., Wed.-Sun., 9 a.m.-5 p.m.
Place: 7 mi. off US 4.
Contact: (802) 273-2282

Glover

Puppets

Hundreds of puppets of all sizes and many varieties of colorful masks are on hand at the Bread and Puppet Museum. You can see a giant washerwoman and an 18-foot green dragon — kids may want to crawl underneath the dragon and see how a dragon belly really looks!

Time: June-Aug., 8 a.m.-5 p.m.; rest of year, by appt. only.
Place: 2 mi S of town on VT 122.
Contact: (802) 525-6972

Grafton

Old Tavern

This historic tavern (built in 1801) was a favorite of Kipling, who stayed here frequently. The tavern is now an inn and restaurant with antique furnishings, paintings and original Currier and Ives prints. A wonderful stop that will put you into the nineteenth century!

Time: 8 a.m.-11 p.m.
Place: Main St.
Contact: (802) 843-2231

Grand Isle

Oldest Log Cabin

Built in 1783 and still in its original condition, the Hyde Log Cabin may be the oldest cabin in the US. There are many antiques and collectibles on display. If you'd like, you can bring a bag lunch and sit in the park area surrounding the cabin.

Time: July-Aug., Wed.-Sun., 9 a.m.-5 p.m.
Place: On US 2.
Contact: (802) 828-3226

Healdville

Premier Cheese

Crowley Cheese makes some of the finest cheese in the state

VERMONT

Healdville

and has been doing so since just after the revolutionary war. A 30-minute tour of the factory (built in 1882) includes a view of the entire cheese-making process. Try to arrive at 11 a.m., the most active time at the plant.

Time: Mon.-Sat., 8 a.m.-4 p.m., by appt. only.
Place: 2 mi. off VT 103, in town.
Contact: (802) 259-2340

Ludlow

Cider Sample

The Green Mountain Sugar House makes maple syrup, maple sugar, maple butter and cider in season. Visitors are welcome, but no formal tours are given. You're encouraged to sample the variety of maple products and cider, which you can buy here at reduced rate.

Time: Syrup production: Mar.-Apr., sunrise to sunset. Cider production: Sept.-Oct., sunrise to sunset.
Place: 4 mi. N of town on VT 100.
Contact: (802) 228-7151

Manchester

Fly Fishing

Hundreds of rods, some owned by famous fly fishermen from Hemingway to Eisenhower, are on display in the Museum of American Fly Fishing. You can also see exhibits on the sport and on its many enthusiasts.

Time: 9 a.m.-5 p.m.
Place: .25 mi. S of town on US 7.
Contact: (802) 362-3300

Middlebury

Walking Tour

Combine your daily exercise with some regional history in a walking tour of 25 of Middlebury's historic buildings. You'll see several churches with the traditional white steeples and many fine examples of early New England architecture. Pick up a free map and guidebook at the contact listed below.

Time: June-Labor Day, Mon.-Fri., 8:30 a.m.-4:30 p.m.; Sat., 10 a.m.-4 p.m.; Sun., noon-4 p.m.
Place: Visitor center, 35 Court St.
Contact: (802) 388-7579

Montpelier

23.75 Carat Gold

On a sunny day, the dome of the State House, covered with 23.75 carat gold leaf, shines like a golden ball of fire! Tours of the 1859 building, the site of the Vermont legislature, come free of charge and last about an hour.

Time: Tours: mid-May-Dec., Mon.-Fri., 8 a.m.-4 p.m.
Place: State St.
Contact: (802) 828-1110

Last Panther

The Vermont Historical Society offers exhibits that give a good overview of the state's history including an exhibit — on the last panther shot in Vermont. You can also see a rare music box-gambling machine, a collection of jewelry made from human hair, clothing originally worn by Ethan Allen and much more.

Time: Sept.-June, Mon.-Fri., 8 a.m.-4:30 p.m. July-Aug., Mon.-Fri., 8 a.m.-4:30 p.m.; Sat.-Sun., 10 a.m.-5 p.m.
Place: 109 State St.
Contact: (802) 828-2291

American Art

In Kellogg-Hubbard Library, the Thomas W. Wood Art Gallery has an excellent collection of early 20th-century American art, as well as a wide variety of changing exhibitions.

Time: Mem. Day-Labor Day, Tues.-Fri., noon-4 p.m.; Sat., 9:30 a.m.-1 p.m. Rest of year, Tues.-Sat., noon-4 p.m.
Place: 135 Main St., at School St.
Contact: (802) 229-0036

Newport

Maple Candies

Arrive in the morning to see candies being made at American Maple Products. The company also offers a free movie on maple sugaring, which is shown aboard a restored 1905 railway passenger coach!
Time: Candies made:
Mon.-Thurs., mid-morning.
Place: On Bluff Rd.
Contact: (802) 334-6516

Plymouth

Free Cheese Samples

Producing cheese from a 19th-century formula, the Plymouth Cheese Corporation offers free samples and a chance to watch the cheese making process. Arrive in the late morning for the best action at the factory.
Time: Tues.-Fri., 8 a.m.-3 p.m.
Place: Just off VT 100A in town.
Contact: (802) 672-3650

Quechee

Little Grand Canyon

The Ottauquechee River has gouged out a gorge which has been nicknamed "Vermont's Little Grand Canyon." From a bridge on US 4, just outside Quechee, you can look 163 feet straight down to its bottom.

The Quechee Gorge river bottom runs for one mile and makes an excellent hike.
Contact: (802) 295-3545 or 295-7900

Ripton

Robert Frost Home

The home and cabin in which this famous poet did much of his writing is open by appointment only. The farm rests on a hill with a lovely view, and the apple orchard blossoms in the spring. Or you may want to come in the winter to see the woods on a snowy evening!
Time: By appt. only.
Place: 2 mi. E of town off VT 125.
Contact: (802) 388-7944 or 388-7579

Rockingham

Picture Perfect

An 1889 soda fountain, an 1872 covered bridge, an 1810 grist mill — these things could be right off a calendar, but here they stand in real life at the Rockingham, Vermont Country Store.
Time: Mon.-Sat., 9 a.m.-5 p.m.
Place: 2.5 mi. W of I-91 on VT 103.
Contact: (802) 463-3855

St. Johnsbury

Art Gallery

The St. Johnsbury Athenaeum Gallery includes excellent examples of the Hudson River school of paintings. You'll get an idea of how the river valleys looked in the days before steamships, railroads and cars.
Time: Mon.-Sat., 9:30 a.m.-5 p.m.
Place: 30 Main St.
Contact: (802) 748-8291

Strafford

Gothic House

The Justin Smith Morrill Homestead, built by a famous Vermont senator, is a large complex of buildings from the nineteenth century, including an unusual Gothic Revival house, six farm buildings and several formal gardens. You can walk around the landscaped grounds or stroll through the buildings at your leisure.
Time: Mid-May-mid-Oct., Tues.-Sun., 9 a.m.-5 p.m.
Place: Main St.
Contact: (802) 828-3226

Townshend

Toy Animals

It takes a lot of stuffing for the Mary Meyer Manufacturing

VERMONT

Townshend

Company to turn out 5,000 toy animals a week. You can watch the stuffing (and a lot of other work) on a 20-minute tour of the company.

Time: Mon.-Fri., 9 a.m.-noon, 1 p.m.-3:30 p.m. Please call 1 day ahead for an appt.
Place: VT 30.
Contact: (802) 365-7793

Waterbury Center

Cider Press

At the Cold Hollow Cider Press you're within five feet of the machinery that grinds the apples; then they are pressed into pure apple cider, at the pace of 1/2 million gallons a year. Free cold cider (or hot spiced in cold months)!

Time: Sept.-May, 8 a.m.-6 p.m.
Place: On VT 100.
Contact: (802) 244-8560

Weston

Woodware

Over 100,000 people stop at Weston Bowl Mill each year to see its woodware collection and to check out the seconds for sale at reduced prices. These might include bowls, lazy susans and even bird feeders. This woodcarving tradition began in 1902 and is still going strong.

Time: June-Sept., 8 a.m.-6 p.m.; rest of year, 10 a.m.-5 p.m.
Place: On VT 100.
Contact: (802) 824-6219

Country Store

The Vermont Country Store in Weston sells rock candy and

calico as it must have when it first opened in 1890. An old-fashioned place in an old-fashioned country village!.

Time: Mon.-Sat., 9 a.m.-5 p.m.
Place: S of the Village Green.
Contact: (802) 824-5432

Wilmington

Queen Bees

Every 15 minutes the Maple Grove Honey Museum features a 12-minute film on the life of honey bees. Not only can you see a hive of bees, but you can also sample several varieties of honey!

Time: 8 a.m.-5 p.m.
Place: 2 mi. N of town on VT 100.
Contact: (802) 464-2193

Windsor

Vermont's Birthplace

The "Birthplace of Vermont" is a tavern, called the "Old Constitution House," in which the Constitution of the Republic of Vermont was signed in 1777. Come here for a glimpse of history.

Time: May 16-Oct. 11, Wed.-Sun., 10 a.m.-5 p.m.
Place: 16 N. Main St.
Contact: (802) 828-3226

Statewide

Maple Orchards

In the late winter and early spring the smell of sap bubbling into maple syrup and sugar draws thousands of visitors to Vermont's many maple orchards and sugar houses. Some charge for tours, but most do not. Almost all sites charge if you want to gather sap in the wooded areas as an outing with family and friends, but a visit to watch the workers produce syrup and sugar is usually great fun —and free! For a list of maple orchards, write to the contact below.

Contact: Vermont Sugarmakers' Association, Attn.: Sandra Ferrier, R.D. 2, Westford, VT 05494.

Covered Bridges

You can see almost 150 covered bridges in this state. A 400-foot covered bridge stretches from Windsor, Vermont to Cornish, New Hampshire. While that may be the longest bridge, one of the most beautiful is in Warren. You've already seen it dozens of times — in Salem cigarette commercials. For a list of all the covered bridges, write to the contact below.

Contact: Vermont State Chamber of Commerce, Box 37, Montpelier, VT 05602.

Scenic Drive

A beautiful drive through the mountains: Smugglers Notch along VT 108 from Stowe to Jeffersonville. You'll see many jagged peaks, large rocks and hardy evergreens along the road leading to this notch made famous by smugglers traveling between New England and Canada.

Scenic Drive

Follow the local road from Cambridge south through Pleasant Valley to Underhill Center for a lovely view of rolling farmland, old-fashioned barns and rambling homesteads. Although the road is unmarked on the map, there's only one leading in that direction, and you'll be delighted by the fine scenery.

Picture Postcard Towns

Vermont's a picturesque state so that picking out some of its picture-postcard towns may seem unfair to dozens not listed. Nevertheless, here are some of the most appealing: Chelsea, Newfane, Peacham, Rupert, Topsham Four Corners, Waits River, West Topsham.

VIRGINIA

ATTRACTIONS·THE BEST FREE
THE BEST FREE ATTRACTIONS·
FREE ATTRACTIONS·THE BEST
ATTRACTIONS·THE BEST FREE
THE BEST FREE ATTRACTIONS·
FREE ATTRACTIONS·THE BEST
ATTRACTIONS·THE BEST FREE

Arlington •

RICHMOND
★

Norfolk •

VIRGINIA

Accotnik

Pohick Church

Founded in 1773, this historic structure was once the parish church of Mount Vernon. George Washington selected the site for the church in 1767 and served as its vestryman for 27 years.

Time: 8 a.m.-4 p.m.
Place: 2 mi. SW of town on US 1.

Alexandria

Stabler-Leadbeater Apothecary Museum

This late 18th-century drugstore was frequented by the likes of George and Martha Washington and Robert E. Lee, and remains in its original condition. The old wooden shelves are stocked with hand-blown glass nursing bottles, "perfection" eyeglasses and many varieties of antique surgical instruments.

Time: Mon.-Sat., 10 a.m.-4:30 p.m.; closed holidays.
Place: 105-107 S. Fairfax St.
Contact: (703) 836-3713

George Washington Bicentennial Center

Two permanent exhibits and several rotating displays present the American Revolution and the history of early plantation life in northern Virginia, through vivid audio-visual commentary. Travel information and a museum gift shop are also at the center.

Time: 9 a.m.-5 p.m.
Place: 201 S. Washington St.
Contact: (703) 750-6677

Washington's Birthday Celebration

Alexandria, the hometown of George Washington, honors his birthday each February with a month-long celebration. The highlight of this event is a gala parade in the city's Old Town district, featuring several fife-and-drum corps, citizens costumed as colonial soldiers and more. Other events can be found all over the city throughout the month.

Contact: (703) 549-0205

Re-fighting the Revolution

One of the most exciting highlights of the month-long Washington's Birthday celebration in Alexandria is the revolutionary war reenactment at Fort Ward Park. Don't miss the mock battle between British and Colonial troops. There's also a fine interpretive program on the life of a typical revolutionary war soldier.

Place: 4301 W. Braddock Rd., about 6 mi. from Washington D.C. via I-395.
Contact: (703) 750-6425
Note: Parking is available on West Braddock Rd.

Fort Stevens Battle Reenacted

Union and Confederate troops clash again during a reenactment of the Battle of Fort Stevens held every August 10 at Fort Ward Park, a 40-acre historic landmark built to protect Washington, D.C. from invasion during the Civil War. The mock battle is part of a two-day Civil War program that includes military unit competition and an authentic war encampment. While here, stop for a picnic on the grounds or walk along the scenic nature trails.

Time: Park: 9 a.m.-sunset. Museum: Tues.-Sat., 9 a.m.-5 p.m.; Sun., noon-5 p.m.

Fort Ward Museum and Park

Located in this 40-acre woodland park is a partial restoration of one of the stone forts built to defend Washington during the Civil War. Those interested in Civil War artifacts should view the cannons, guns and costumes in the Civil War Museum. Interpretive programs are offered in the summer—ask about free concerts.

Time: Park: 9 a.m.-sunset. Museum: Tues.-Sat., 9 a.m.-5 p.m.; Sun., noon-5 p.m. Concerts: mid-May-mid-Sept., Thurs., 7:45 p.m.

Place: 4301 W. Braddock Rd., between King St. and Seminary Rd., just E of I-395.

Contact: (703) 750-6425

Mount Vernon Trail

The 17-mile Mount Vernon Trail runs alongside the Potomac River and George Washington Memorial Parkway from Mount Vernon to the Lincoln Memorial in Washington D.C. Walk, jog or ride your bike past such sites as Fort Hunt Park, Dyke Marsh Wildlife Habitat, a 19th-century lighthouse at Jones Point Park, Lady Bird Johnson Park and the Arlington Memorial Bridge. You might also want to have a picnic on the grass along the way.

Contact: Superintendent, George Washington Memorial Parkway, Turkey Run Park, McLean VA 22101; (703) 426-6600

Christ Church

George Washington and Robert E. Lee both worshipped in this historic church, which has remained virtually unchanged since its construction in the 1770s. Some of the unusual features of the church include the "wine glass" pulpit (shaped like a delicate glass) and the beautiful chandeliers.

Time: Mon.-Fri., 9:30 a.m.-5 p.m.; Sat., 9 a.m.-noon; Sun., 2-4:30 p.m.

Place: 118 N. Washington St., at the corner of Washington and Columbus.

Contact: (703) 549-1450

George Washington Masonic National Memorial

From its site high above the Potomac River, this 333-foot high shrine commands a view of Alexandria at its feet and Washington six miles distant. Inside are numerous "secret" meeting rooms and a chair from which George Washington presided. Children will appreciate the 28-foot long musical toy parade with platoons of nobles marching to recorded band music.

Time: 9:15 a.m.-4 p.m.

Place: King St. and Callahan Dr.

Contact: (703) 683-2007

Arlington

The Pentagon

The Pentagon is the world's biggest office building. Some

27,000 people work here in rooms flanking mile-long corridors often filled with bike-riding messengers. Contained in this famous building are the offices of the armed forces chief, the secretary of defense and colorful displays of trophies, medals, uniforms and battle-action photos.

Time: Mon.-Fri., 7 a.m.-6 p.m.

Place: Across 14th St. Bridge.

Contact: (202) 695-1776

Tomb of the Unknown Soldier

Buried under this famous tomb is the body of an unknown soldier brought back from France after World War I.

VIRGINIA

Arlington

The striking sculpture is carved from a piece of Colorado-Yule marble, one of the largest blocks ever quarried. Also buried here are the remains of unknown American soldiers who died in World War II and the Korean War. Selected members of the military guard the tomb 24 hours a day. The changing of the guard is a ritual worth seeing.
Time: Cemetery: Oct. -Mar. 8 a.m.-5 p.m.; Apr.-Sept., 8 a.m.-7 p.m. Changing of the guard: every half hour during summer; every hour during winter.
Place: Arlington National Cemetery.
Contact: (202) 692-0931

Kennedy Graves

Each year thousands visit the grave of John F. Kennedy, marked by an eternal flame. Adjacent is the gravesite of Robert F. Kennedy.
Time: Oct.-Mar., 8 a.m.-5 p.m.; Apr.-Sept., 8 a.m.-7 p.m.
Place: Arlington National Cemetery.
Contact: (202) 692-0931

Marine Corps War Memorial

At the north end of the cemetery, overlooking the Capital stands this famous memorial depicting the flag-raising at Iwo Jima. Modeled after Joseph Rosenthal's photo, this statue stands 78 feet high and weighs 100 tons. Don't miss the color ceremony and drill by a platoon of marines—and hear a half-hour taped concert of the 49 Netherland bells.
Time: Color ceremony: June 1- Aug. 31, Tues., 7:30 p.m.
Place: Arlington National Cemetery.
Contact: (202) 692-0931

Arlington House

Visit this beautifully restored mansion overlooking the Potomac and the Capital, where Robert E. Lee courted and married Mary Ann Randolph Curtis. They lived here from 1831 to 1861. Because of its location, Union troops occupied the house during the Civil War. It is a 12-minute walk from Arlington Cemetery Visitor Center.
Time: Apr.-Sept., 9:30 a.m.-6 p.m.; rest of year, 9:30 a.m.-4:30 p.m.
Place: Arlington National Cemetery.
Contact: (202) 692-0931

Netherlands Carillon Tower

This striking tower and its 49 bells were a gift from the Netherlands in gratitude for the aid given by the US during and after World War II. Live concerts are performed throughout the year.
Time: Concerts: Sat. and holidays, 2 p.m.
Place: Outside Arlington National Cemetery, on Ridge Rd. off US 50.
Contact: (703) 827-0741

Big Stone Gap

Early Virginia Life

The Southwest Virginia Museum and Historical State Park contain various items and dioramas depicting the history and activities of southwestern Virginia, including pioneer furnishings, folk art and culture and miniature log houses.
Time: Tues.-Sat., 9:30 a.m.-5 p.m.; Sun., 2-5 p.m.
Place: W. First St. and Wood Ave.
Contact: (703) 523-1322

Charlottesville

University of Virginia

Founded by Thomas Jefferson in 1817, this impressive university also bears the stamp of his architectural genius. Many of the old buildings were modeled after classical models, in particular the Rotunda after the Pantheon in Rome. Even more noteworthy is the plan of the quadrangle, which originally housed both students and faculty, and the connecting arcade which wraps the space. The rooms of such famed former students as Edgar Allan Poe and Woodrow Wilson are preserved for public viewing. A Museum of Fine Arts is another attraction on campus.

Time: Mon.-Fri., 11 a.m.-3 p.m.; Sat., 11 a.m., 2 and 4 p.m.; no tours mid-May-mid-Sept., mid-Dec.-mid-Jan. or during exams.
Place: On US 29 and 250 business routes.

Chincoteague

Wallops Flight Center

NASA's Wallops Island facility is a launch site for small rockets and satellites. Tours of the site include a range control center, rocket launching facilities and an orientation movie.

Time: June-Aug., Mon.-Fri., by appt. only.
Place: 3.5 mi. E of US 13 on VA 175.
Contact: (804) 824-3411

National Wildlife Refuge

Whistling swans, three-foot high Sitka Deer, wild horses and 250 varieties of birds—including egrets, herons and ibises—frequent this natural wildlife wonderland. Swimming and surfing facilities are available in the area.

Place: Take Madox Blvd. to far end of town and cross bridge to the refuge on Assateague Island.
Contact: (804) 336-6122

Annual Pony Penning

Once a year, as part of a volunteer fireman's carnival, Chincoteague ponies are herded into the Assateague channel for a short swim to Chincoteague, where they are auctioned on the carnival

grounds. (The event was the basis for the children's classic, *Misty of Chincoteague*.) The mares and stallions not purchased are released to swim back to their island refuge.

Time: Pony swims: last week of July, in the morning, depending on the tide. Carnival: late July-early Aug., Mon.-Sat., 7:30 a.m.-noon.
Contact: President, Chincoteague Volunteer Fire Department, Chincoteague, VA 23336; Chamber of Commerce, (804) 336-6161.

Danville

Harvest Jubilee

This celebration of Danville's Victorian history is held in late September in the city's warehouse district. Victorian-style vendors, artists and craftsmen line the streets, peddling wares and vittles. Tours are conducted of Danville's Victorian homes and the National Tobacco Textile Museum. Victorian music, a parade of years, and antique displays are also featured.

Time: 2nd weekend in Sept.
Contact: Harvest Jubilee, Chairperson, P.O. Box 3300, Danville, VA 24541; (804) 799-5200.

VIRGINIA

Fort Belvoir

US Army Engineer Museum

Exhibits in this interesting museum trace the 200-year history of the US Army Corps of Engineers. Also on display are a map of the 1781 Battle of Yorktown, engineering models, presidential letters, paintings and flags.

Time: Mon.-Fri., 8 a.m.-4:30 p.m., Sat., 1-4 p.m.
Place: 16th and Belvoir Rd.
Contact: (202) 664-6104

Fort Lee

US Army Quartermaster Museum

One of the nation's finest military museums, it includes an arsenal of battle weapons, arrays of uniforms and decorations dating from 1775, and a century-old saddlemaker shop.

Time: Mon.-Fri., 8 a.m.-5 p.m.; Sat., Sun. and holidays, 11 a.m.-5 p.m.
Place: 2 mi. E of Petersburg.
Contact: US Army Quartermaster Museum, Fort Lee, VA 23801; (804) 734-4203.

Fredericksburg

Union Headquarters

This 18th-century mansion, Chatham Manor, served as a hospital during the Civil War. Union soldiers stayed here before crossing the river to fight the Battle of Fredericksburg. Today it boasts of beautiful rose gardens and a collection of Civil War memorabilia.

Time: 9 a.m.-5 p.m.
Place: 1 mi. E of town off VA 218.
Contact: (703) 373-9400

A Dog Day Afternoon

One day each year, Fredericksburg literally "goes to the dogs," as the Dog Mart, a 283-year-old celebration, fills the streets of the city. Highlights of the day include a dog auction; contests for the ugliest, best-dressed and funniest dogs; and a canine parade. For variety, the festival also includes band and fiddle music, Indian dancing, turkey- and hog-calling contests and foxhorn blowing.

Time: 1st Sat. in Oct.
Place: Downtown Fredericksburg.
Contact: (703) 373-1776

National Military Park

The Chancellorsville battlefield is one of four major Civil War battlefields in the Fredericksburg and Spotsylvania National Military Park. The Battles of Chancellorsville and Salem Church, fought here May 1-6, 1863, were among the most important engagements of the Civil War. Two visitor center museums feature exhibits and a documentary film. Special summer programs interpret military life and other Civil War themes.

Time: 9 a.m.-5 p.m.
Place: Lafayette Blvd. (US 1) and Sunlen Rd.
Contact: Fredericksburg and Spotslvania National Military Park, Fredericksburg, VA 22401; P.O. Box 679; (703) 373-4461

Hampton

Army Transportation Museum

The US Army Transportation Museum at Fort Eustis features an exhibit of the historical progress of military transportation since the revolutionary war, including a captive "flying saucer."

Time: Mon.-Fri., 8 a.m.-5 p.m.; Sun., noon-5 p.m.
Contact: P.O. Drawer D, Fort Eustis, VA 23604; (804) 878-3603.

Moon Rocks and More

Langley Air Force Base is headquarters for the Tactical Air Command and the laboratories of the NASA Langely Research Center and Visitor Center. Among the special attractions at the Visitor Center are exhibits of moon rock, a space suit, the Apollo 12 Command Module and other examples of aeronautics and space research. Movies are also shown.

Time: Mon.-Sat., 8:30 a.m.-4:30 p.m.; Sun., noon-4:30 p.m.
Contact: Langley Research Center, Hampton, VA 23665; (804) 827-2855.

Bluebird Gap Farm

Children can pet the farm animals here, and can view various fowl, farm machinery and a barn. Contains picnic and play areas.

Time: Wed.-Sun., 9 a.m.-5 p.m.
Place: On Pine Chapel Rd. between I-64 and Queen St.
Contact: (804) 727-6347

Hardy

Booker T. Washington National Monument

Embracing 224 acres, this monument is a partial recrea- tion of the tobacco plantation on which Booker T. Washington was born as a slave. A visitor center features exhibits and a movie on Washington's life. Living history demonstrations are presented by costumed interpreters and farm animals of the 1860s can be seen from the self-guiding trail. Have a picnic on the grounds.

Time: Visitor center: 8:30 a.m.-5 p.m. Living history: mid-June-Labor Day, 8:30 a.m.-5 p.m.
Place: 20 mi. SE of Roanoke via VA 116 S to Burnt Chimney, then VA 122.
Contact: Rt. 1, Box 195, Hardy, VA 24101; (703) 721-2094.

Hopewell

Beautiful Wayside

CBS television newsman Charles Kuralt once called these gardens "America's most beautiful wayside." Created and privately maintained by the late Walter H. Misenheimer in a natural wooded setting, the gardens and boxwood-lined trails display colorful glimpses of dogwood, camellias, azaleas and delicate wild flowers.

Time: Best in azalea season, mid-to late-Apr.
Place: VA 10, 21 mi. E of Hopewell.

Contact: Mac Eubank, (804) 458-5536.
Note: Mr. Misenheimer tried unsuccessfully to deed his wayside to the State of Virginia, but the gift was declined and thus remains private property. Please leave it as you find it.

Keswick

The Blessing of the Hounds

Ever since 1928, the Blessing of the Hounds service has been held at Grace Church on Thanksgiving Day. The Keswick Hunt Club and members of other hunt clubs participate. The service is held outdoors where the horses, dogs and uniformed riders gather for blessings before they start the hunt, usually on a farm adjacent to church property.

Contact: Grace Episcopal Church, Box 43, Keswick, VA 22947; (804) 293-3549

Lexington

Steele's Tavern

The Cyrus McCormick Memorial Museum and Wayside in the village of Steele's Tavern is a shrine to the American inventor Cyrus McCormick. More than a dozen miniature model

VIRGINIA

Lexington

reapers, threshers, and bellows as well as a restored blacksmith shop, gristmill and slave quarters are on display. The farm and workshop where McCormick invented the reaper that revolutionized the world's agriculture is nearby. Picnic facilities are available.

Time: Mid-Apr.-mid-Oct., 8 a.m.-5 p.m. Rest of year, by appt.
Place: 20 mi. N of town on US 11.
Contact: (804) 377-2255

Lee's Chapel

Built in 1867 under the supervision of Robert E. Lee, the Lee Chapel and Museum sits on the campus of Washington and Lee University, where Lee served as president. It contains Lee's office and family crypt, a statue of Lee, and the famous Custis Family Portrait Collection. The shrine is a National Historic Landmark.

Time: Mid-Oct.-mid-Apr., Mon.-Sat., 9 a.m.-4 p.m.; Sun., 2-5 p.m. Mid-Apr.-mid-Oct., Mon-Sat., 9 a.m.-5 p.m.; Sun., 2-5 p.m.
Place: On the campus of Washington and Lee University near Jefferson and Washington Sts.
Contact: (703) 463-9111, ext. 289

Virginia Military Institute

Known as "the West Point of the South," VMI was founded in 1839 and is the oldest state-supported military college in the nation. Stonewall Jackson taught here and General George C. Marshall was a 1901 graduate. Officially designated a National Historic District, VMI houses a museum containing Stonewall Jackson and George S. Patton mementos, a planetarium and the George Marshall Research Library.

Time: Mon.-Fri., 9 a.m.-4:30 p.m.; Sat., 9 a.m.-noon and 2-5 p.m.; Sun., 2-5 p.m.
Place: Museum: Jackson Memorial Hall.
Contact: Virginia Military Institute, Lexington, VA 24450; (703) 463-6232.

Dress Parade

Every Tuesday and Friday at 4:20 p.m. during fall and spring semesters, cadets of Virginia Military Institute march in full-dress parade. Guard mounts are conducted at 12:30 p.m. on those days.

Contact: (703) 463-6232

Goshen Pass

This breathtaking mountain gorge, formed by the Maury River, is ideal for picnicking, swimming, sightseeing or quiet relaxation.

Place: 15 mi. NE of Lexington via US 11 and VA 39.

Historic Walking Tour

Robert E. Lee's office, Stonewall Jackson's home and George C. Marshall's Nobel Peace Prize are among the highlights you'll see during a two-hour guided walking tour of historic Lexington. Take your pick of three self-guided tours: the Lee-Jackson Walking Tour, the VMI-Marshall Tour, and the Residential Tour. Excellent free brochures are provided.

Time: Tours: Apr. 1-Oct. 31, Mon.-Sat., 10 a.m.; Sun., 2 p.m.
Contact: Historic Lexington Visitor Center, Sloan House, 107 E. Washington St., Lexington, VA 24450; (703) 463-3777.

George C. Marshall Museum

Located on the west edge of the Virginia Military Institute Parade Ground, this museum traces Marshall's career, with particular emphasis on the years of the two world wars and the Marshall Plan. An audio-visual presentation traces the developments of World War II.

Time: Apr. 16-Oct. 14, Mon-Sat., 10 a.m.-4 p.m.; Sun., 2-5 p.m. Rest of year, Mon.-Sat., 10 a.m.-4 p.m.; Sun., 2-5 p.m.

Contact: Virginia Military Institute, P.O. Box 920, Lexington, VA 24450; (703) 463-7103.

Luray

Singing Tower

Situated in a beautiful park and garden, Luray Carillon Tower is 117 feet tall, 25 feet square at the base and contains 47 bells, the largest of which weighs 7,640 pounds. Regular concert recitals by famed Carillonneurs are best heard from a distance of 200-300 yards.

Time: Recitals: June 1-Sept. 14, Tues., Thurs., Sat. and Sun., 8 p.m.; Mar. 1-May 31 and Sept. 16-Oct. 30, 2 p.m. Additional recitals on Easter and Labor Day.

Place: 1 mi. W of town on US 211 at entrance to Luray Caverns.

Manassas

Bull Run Battle Site

Two great Civil War battles, the First and Second Battles of Manassas, also known as the two Battles of Bull Run, were fought here. The national Battlefield Park Visitor Center offers a museum and slide show program, and a three-dimensional map presents strategies of both battles. Also of interest is the Stone House, renovated as a Civil War field hospital.

Time: Grounds: 9 a.m.-dark. Visitor Center: Summer, 9 a.m.-6 p.m.; rest of year, 9 a.m.-5:30 p.m. The Stone House: June 15-Labor Day, 10 a.m.-5 p.m.

Place: On VA 234 near jct. of US 29/211.

Contact: Manassas National Battlefield Park, P.O. Box 1830, Manassas, VA 22110; (703) 754-7107.

McLean

Turkey Run Farm

This 100-acre farm and the hand-built cabin on its premises depict the daily life of a small family of the 1770s. Special evening programs feature country dances as well as 18th-century music and games.

Time: Apr. 1-Nov. 30, Wed.-Sun., 10 a.m.-4:30 p.m.; rest of year, Fri.-Sun., 10 a.m.-4:30 p.m. Evening programs: Apr.-Sept., second Thurs. of month.

Place: Exit 13 off I-495, then 2.25 mi. E on VA 193. Turn left

and follow signs.
Contact: (703) 557-1356

Middleburg

Meredyth Vineyards

Individuals and groups are invited to tour this winery located in the historic foothills of the Bull Run Mountains, 90 minutes away from the nation's capital. The 30-minute guided tour culminates in a tasting session.

Contact: P.O. Box 347, Middleburg, VA 22117; (703) 687-6612.

Norfolk

Chrysler Museum

The Chrysler Museum's collection is one of the most important and comprehensive art assemblages in the US. Art treasures from every period of civilization and by virtually all of the masters of fine and decorative arts are on display. The museum's glass collection is one of the finest in the world. Visitors will want to browse through the gift shop and enjoy performing arts in the theater.

Time: Tues.-Sat., 10 a.m.-4 p.m.; Sun., 1-5 p.m.
Place: 3 blocks W of Olney Rd. and Virginia Beach Blvd.
Contact: (703) 622-1211

VIRGINIA

Norfolk

MacArthur Memorial

Housed in a city courthouse built in 1847, the MacArthur Memorial contains an extensive collection of exhibits and memorabilia tracing General Douglas MacArthur's controversial life and military career. There are nine galleries of displays that include the general's famous corncob pipe, the surrender documents that ended World War II, his 1950 staff car and a reconstruction of two of his offices. A continuous 22-minute film shows highlights of his life.

Time: Mon.-Sat., 10 a.m.-5 p.m.; Sun., 11 a.m.-5 p.m.
Place: City Hall Ave.
Contact: (804) 441-2382

Azalea Festival

Some 250,000 azaleas line 12 miles of paths in Norfolk during the annual International Azalea Festival held in late April. Norfolk's yearly salute to the North Atlantic Treaty Organization, the celebration combines dance, art and athletic tournaments into a week-long event that culminates with the Grand Parade through downtown and the queen's coronation in the beautiful Gardens by the Sea.

Time: Late April.
Contact: Norfolk Chamber of Commerce, 420 Bank St., Norfolk, VA 23501; (804) 622-2312.

St. Paul's Church

Built in 1739, St. Paul's Church was the lone survivor of the British bombardment of

Norfolk in 1776. A cannonball fired during that battle is still embedded in the southeastern wall of the church. Traditional services are still held here.

Time: Tues.-Sat., 10 a.m.-4 p.m.; Sun., 2-4 p.m. Services: Sun., 8 and 11 a.m.
Contact: (703) 627-4353

Harborfest

Tall ships, fireworks, roaring cannons and shouting pirates signal the celebration of Norfolk's annual Harborfest weekend each spring. The three-day waterfront festival features a variety of aquatic events and is climaxed by a Pirate's Ball at the Norfolk Boatbuilding School.

Time: Late May.
Contact: Norfolk Convention and Visitors Bureau, P.O. Box 238, Scope Plaza, Norfolk, VA 23501; (804) 441-5266.
Note: There is a nominal admission fee to the Pirate's Ball.

Petersburg

Siege Museum

A stunning Greek Revival structure, originally built as a tobacco and merchandise exchange, now houses the Siege Museum. Inside, displays and vivid audio-visual presentations depict conditions during the 10-month Civil War siege of Petersburg, the longest such siege in American history.

Time: Mon.-Sat., 9 a.m.-5 p.m.; Sun., 1-5 p.m.
Place: 15 W. Bank St.
Contact: Siege Museum, 15 W. Bank St., Petersburg, VA. 23803; (804) 861-2904.

Trapezium House

One of the most unique houses in Petersburg, this architectural oddity was built around 1817 by an eccentric Irish bachelor, Charles O'Hara. The story goes that O'Hara was convinced by a West Indian servant that a house with right angles would harbor evil spirits, so he ordered his home built in the form of a trapezoid, or trapezium—with no parallel sides and no right angles. A restoration of the house is soon to be completed.

Time: Mon.-Sat., 9 a.m.-5 p.m.; Sun., 1-5 p.m. Open as restoration permits.
Place: 244 Market St.
Contact: (804) 861-8080

Historic Mansion

Civil War relics abound in the Centre Hill Mansion Museum in Petersburg. On display are such items as General Grant's furniture and wagons used by General Sherman on his march through Georgia. Elegant federal chandeliers and mid-19th-century music recreate the ambience of the period.

Time: Mon.-Sat., 9 a.m.-5 p.m.; Sun., 1-5 p.m.
Place: Centre Hill Court, off Franklin St.
Contact: (804) 732-8081

Tobacco Plant Tour

You'll see the whole story of tobacco—from seed to smoke—during a tour of the Brown and Williamson Tobacco Corporation. A highlight of the tour is the chance to watch whirring machines swallow tobacco and paper and spit out cigarettes in split-seconds. Also offered is an audio-visual presentation on the cultivation of the crop.

Time: Mon.-Fri., 8:30 a.m.-4 p.m.
Place: 325 Brown St.
Contact: (804) 732-5222, ext. 232
Note: Tours are for individuals and groups of 15 visitors or less. Larger groups may arrange tours by calling in advance.

Farmers Bank

Memories of the antebellum days of finance and trade come to life in one of the oldest known bank buildings in America. See and hear an audio-visual account of early American banking inside the old double vault. Witness the actual press and plates once used to print the bank's own brand of money.

Time: Mon.-Sat., 9 a.m.-5 p.m.; Sun., 1-5 p.m.
Place: 19 Bollingbrook St., at Cockade Alley.
Contact: (804) 861-1590

National Battlefield

This 1,531-acre park has been established to commemorate the ten-month Siege of Petersburg during the Civil War, the longest siege any American city has ever endured. Touring this historic area, you'll see and hear a complete account of the Siege, view the site of the famous Battle of the Crater, and come upon other points of interest, including a museum of battlefield weapons and uniforms. Every summer, local college students don Blue and Gray outfits to recreate 1860s life on this battlefield.

Time: Mid-June-Labor Day, 8 a.m.-7 p.m.; rest of year, 8 a.m.-5 p.m.
Place: E of town on VA 36.
Contact: Petersburg National Battlefield, P.O. Box 549, Petersburg, VA 23803; (804) 732-3531.

Church Tiffany Windows

One of America's most beautiful art treasures is housed in the Old Blandford Church in Petersburg. The church is the only building in America to have had its every window—15 in all—designed by Louis C. Tiffany, the master of Art Nouveau. Originally built in 1734,

VIRGINIA

Petersburg

the church was restored as a Confederate shrine in 1901.
Time: Mon.-Sat., 9 a.m.-5 p.m.; Sun., noon-5 p.m.
Place: 319 S. Crater Rd.
Contact: (804) 732-2230

Quartermaster Museum

From revolutionary war canteens to General George Patton's jeep, this unusual museum contains a variety of items associated with the Quartermaster Corps that has fed, housed, clothed and supplied American troops for almost 200 years.
Time: Mon.-Fri., 8 a.m.-5 p.m.; Sat., Sun., 1-5 p.m.
Place: Fort Lee, on VA 36.
Contact: (804) 734-1854

Portsmouth

Lightship Museum

This Coast Guard museum is built into an actual lightship. Exhibits include Coast Guard equipment and realistically fitted quarters of the officers and crew, as well as historic artifacts of Coast Guard lightships of the past century.
Time: Tues.-Sat., 10 a.m.-4:45 p.m.; Sun., 2-4:45 p.m.
Place: London Slip at Water St.

Contact: Lightship Museum, London Slip at Water St., Portsmouth, VA 23704; (804) 393-8741.

Naval History Museum

Located on the Elizabeth River waterfront, the Portsmouth Naval Shipyard Museum displays numerous ship models, uniforms and historic flags. Special attractions are the original *Merrimac* and a Polaris missile.
Time: Tues.-Sat., 10 a.m.-5 p.m.; Sun., 2-5 p.m.
Place: 2 High St.
Contact: Portsmouth Naval Shipyard Museum, P.O. Box 248, 2 High St., Portsmouth, VA 23705; (804) 393-8591.

Richmond

Confederate Capital

This National Battlefield Park commemorates those battles waged to defend the confederate capital. Landmarks from the famous Battle of Cold Harbor and other historic Civil War confrontations are preserved and maintained here. Offers an audio-visual program and exhibits on battles in the Richmond area. See also the exhibits in the Fort Harrison Visitor Center.
Time: Park: 8:30 a.m.-5 p.m. Visitor center and headquar-

ters: 9 a.m.-5 p.m. Fort Harrison Visitor Center: June-Aug., 9:30 a.m.-5:30 p.m.; Apr.-May and Sept.-Oct., Sat.-Sun. only.
Place: 3215 E. Broad St.
Contact: (804) 795-1115

Dogwood Dell Amphitheater

Free ballet, opera and musical plays are held on summer evenings at this lake-studded sanctuary. Carillon concerts chime forth daily. Seats about 2,000.
Place: Byrd Park.
Contact: (804) 780-8686

Maymont Park

This 105-acre, turn-of-the-century estate features a Nature Center, a Victorian-Edwardian museum house, Japanese and Italian gardens and domestic and wild animal exhibits. Children will love the family of bears.
Time: Park: Apr.-Oct., 10 a.m.-7 p.m.; Nov.-Mar., 10 a.m.-5 p.m. Exhibits: Apr.-Oct., Tues.-Sat., 11 a.m.-5 p.m.; Sun., noon-6 p.m. Nov.-Mar., Tues.-Sun., noon-4:30 p.m.
Place: Hampton St. and Pennsylvania Ave.
Contact: 1700 Hampton St., Richmond, VA 23220; (804) 358-7166.

St. John's Church

This quaint frame church was built in 1741 and is the site of

Patrick Henry's famous "Give me liberty . . ." speech which ignited the American Revolution. Reenactments of the speech can be heard on special occasions.

Time: Tours: Feb.-Nov., 10 a.m.-4 p.m. Services: Sun., 11 a.m.
Place: 25th at Broad St.
Contact: St. John's Episcopal Church, 25th at Broad St., Richmond, VA 23223; (804) 795-1300.
Note: Donations accepted. Off-hour tours for groups of 30 or more, 50 cents each.

Bejeweled Eggs

The Virginia Museum of Fine Arts contains galleries filled with everything from jeweled Russian Easter Eggs and Egyptian gold to Renaissance and Impressionist paintings.

Time: Tues.-Sat., 11 a.m.-5 p.m.; Sun., 1-5 p.m.
Place: Boulevard and Grove Aves.
Contact: (804) 257-0844

Restored Homes

More than 300 19th-century homes have been restored in this historic eight-block area called Church Hill—the oldest part of the city. The history of this area, which surrounds Old St. John's Church, includes an Indian massacre of an early English settlement.

Contact: (804) 358-5511

State Capitol

Designed by Thomas Jefferson, the Roman temple-like Virginia State Capitol is the first public example of neo-classical architecture and is the second oldest working capitol in the US. The legislators who meet here now represent the world's oldest English-speaking legislative body with an uninterrupted history. In the rotunda is a statue of George Washington, the only one he ever posed for.

Time: Apr. 1-Nov. 30, 9 a.m.-5 p.m.; rest of year, Mon.-Sat.,
9 a.m.-5 p.m.; Sun., 1-5 p.m.
Place: Capitol Sq., 9th and Grace St.
Contact: The Capitol of Virginia, 9th and Grace St., Richmond, VA 23219; (804) 786-4344.

Roanoke

Scenic Drive

The Blue Ridge Parkway, a 469-mile scenic motorway, connects Shenandoah National Park in Virginia and the Great Smoky Mountains National Park in North Carolina and Tennessee. Following the crest of the Blue Ridge at heights from 649 to 6,053 feet, the road overlooks picturesque panoramas of the Southern Highlands. Among the most interesting sites are Humpback Rocks, James River Wayside, Peaks of Otter and Mabry Mill. Food, lodging and recreational facilities are available along the way.

Contact: Blue Ridge Pkwy., P.O. Box 1710, Roanoke, VA 24008; (703) 982-6213.
Note: Parkway is open all year but sections of the road may be closed in icy or snowy weather. The speed limit of 45 mph is strictly enforced. It is advisable to keep gas tanks at least half-filled.

VIRGINIA

Staunton

Summer Band Concerts

Gypsy Hill Park on Churchville Avenue is the site of summer band concerts every Monday night in Staunton. A special concert by the Statler Brothers is held on the Fourth of July.
Contact: (703) 886-8435

Virginia Beach

Psychic Research Center

A library containing 12,000 psychic readings of the mystic, Edgar Cayce, is the featured attraction at the Association for Research and Enlightenment in Virginia Beach. In addition, free lectures on the world of clairvoyance are presented every other Sunday afternoon at 3:30 in the fall, winter and spring. In summer, frequent lectures and experiments are open to the public.
Time: Library: 9 a.m.-5 p.m. Call ahead for lecture schedule. Center: Mon.-Sat., 9 a.m.-10 p.m.; Sun., 1-10 p.m.
Place: 67 Atlantic St.
Contact: (804) 428-3588

Native Lotus

The last substantial growth of rare native American lotus can be seen here in late July and early August. Seeds from these yellow-blossomed water plants have been sent as far away as Japan.
Place: Saudbridge, 10 mi. S of town.
Contact: (804) 425-7511

Oldest Lighthouse

The oldest lighthouse in the United States, dating back to 1791, can be found within the Fort Story Army Post next to the Cape Henry Memorial. Visitors' passes to enter Fort Story are issued at the East Gate, north end of Atlantic Avenue, or at the West Gate on US 60.
Contact: (804) 425-7511

Wakefield

Washington's Birthplace

On the south side of the Potomac River 38 miles from Fredericksburg is a reproduction of the plantation where George Washington was born. The 538-acre site, known as Wakefield, includes a monument built of old brick on the location of the original Washington home, which burned in 1779. Many of the Washington family furnishings are among the 18th-century antiques in the memorial mansion. Outside, the Colonial Living Farm recreates farm scenes of Washington's boyhood.
Time: 9 a.m.-5 p.m.
Place: 38 mi. E of Fredericksburg off VA 3.
Contact: (804) 224-0196

Williamsburg

Anheuser Busch Hospitality Center

During a visit to the Anheuser Busch Hospitality Center, you can see a color film about the brewery's famous Clydesdale horses and the history of beer. Or you can tour a gallery of Williamsburg area archaeological treasures, stroll through a sunlit courtyard, or peruse the gift shop.
Time: 9 a.m.-4 p.m.
Place: 5 mi. E of Williamsburg on VA 60; then follow the signs to the parking lot.
Contact: (804) 253-3036

Walking Tour

Take a free walk around historic Williamsburg and follow the footsteps of American history. Among the attractions awaiting you en route are the Wren Building, the oldest

continuously used structure in the US, a courthouse built in 1770, picturesque William and Mary College and the Abby Aldrich Rockefeller Art Museum. It's a hike well worth the effort.
Contact: (804) 229-1000

Large Folk Art Collection

The Abby Aldrich Rockefeller Folk Art Center offers the largest collection of American primitive paintings and other art objects in the U.S.—some 1,300 in all. Presented to colonial Williamsburg by Mrs. John D. Rockefeller, Jr., the center is housed in a 19th-century building next to the Williamsburg Inn.
Time: Apr.-Dec., noon-8 p.m.; Jan.-Mar., noon-6 p.m.
Place: 307 S. England St.
Contact: (804) 229-1000, ext. 2424

Yorktown

Yorktown Battlefield

The Colonial National Historical Park, overlooking the historic York River, offers a self-guided tour through the battle fields where the British Army surrendered to George Washington's troops on Oct. 19, 1781. You'll pass fighting lines and historic houses. A museum in the Visitor Center contains exhibits and audio-visual presentations.
Time: 8:30 a.m.-sunset.
Place: 1.5 mi. S of town at the end of Colonial Pkwy.
Contact: Colonial National Historical Park, P.O. Box 210, Yorktown, VA 23690; (804) 898-3400.

Celebrate Yorktown

The surrender of the British at the Battle of Yorktown will be celebrated throughout this town at city parks, historic homes and restored battle-fields. Call the contact for details on events, which include art exhibits, theatrical presentations, military and water-front events, fireworks, entertainment, guest speakers and battle reenactments.
Contact: (804) 898-7229

Statewide

Beaches

Along the Atlantic Coast, Virginia is flanked by beaches with fine sand and tidewater that is just right for swimming, surfing and fishing. Two of these are free to visitors — Virginia Beach and Ocean View in Norfolk. Virginia Beach is a narrow strip of sand noted for its resort hotel and popular night spots as well as for its beach-related activity.
Contact: (804) 786-4484
Note: Salt-water fishing is free from the numerous public beaches.

WEST VIRGINIA

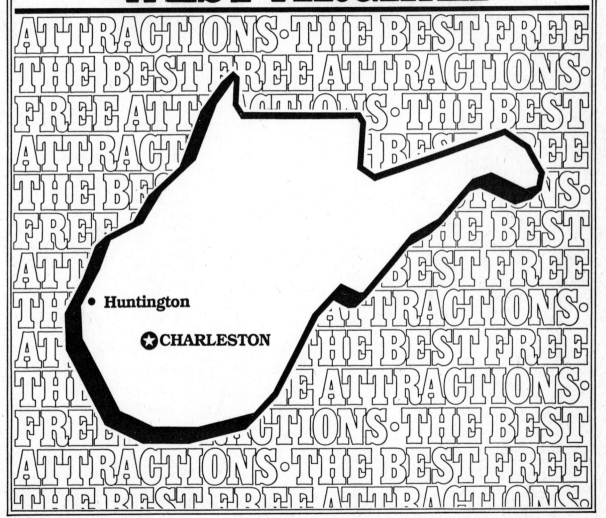

ATTRACTIONS·THE BEST FREE
THE BEST FREE ATTRACTIONS·
FREE ATTRACTIONS·THE BEST
ATTRACTIONS·THE BEST FREE
THE BEST FREE ATTRACTIONS·
FREE ATTRACTIONS·THE BEST
ATTRACTIONS·THE BEST FREE
THE BEST FREE ATTRACTIONS·
FREE ATTRACTIONS·THE BEST
ATTRACTIONS·THE BEST FREE
THE BEST FREE ATTRACTIONS·

• Huntington

★ CHARLESTON

WEST VIRGINIA

Arnoldsburg

Molasses Festival

Square dancing, country music, gospel singing and honest-to-goodness home-made molasses (20 gallons boiled in pans to make one gallon of sweet dark-brown syrup)—a terrific way to spend a September weekend!
Time: Last weekend in Sept.
Place: West Fork Community Park.
Contact: (304) 655-8652

Beckley

Whitewater Rapids

The New River Gorge National River is one of the most popular and thrilling stretches of water in the country. It takes two days to negotiate the 30 miles of whitewater, which vary from difficult to extremely dangerous.
Time: Early Apr.-Nov.
Contact: New River Travel Council, 106-1/2 S. Fayette St., Beckley, WV 25801; (304) 255-6949.
Note: Difficulty of rapids varies with the season.

Berkeley Springs

Apple Butter Festival

Besides old-time apple butter making, there's a farmers market, country and bluegrass music, a beard contest and even turtle races—all of which add up to a delightful fall getaway!
Time: Mid-Oct.
Place: Berkeley Springs State Park.
Contact: (304) 258-3738

Ceredo

Glassblowing

At Pilgrim Glass Corporation you'll have a chance to see the fascinating and fiery art of forming objects through glassblowing. Glass-making has been a tradition here since 1608.
Time: Mon.-Sat., 9 a.m.-5 p.m.; Sun., noon-5 p.m.
Place: Near Airport off I-64.
Contact: (304) 453-3553

Charleston

Thrilling Victories

Press a button to relive the milestones in track history, moments such as Roger Bannister's speeding his way to a 4-minute mile. And enjoy the many displays of the National Track and Field Hall of Fame.
Time: Mon.-Fri., 9 a.m.-4:30 p.m.; Sat., 9 a.m.-5 p.m.; Sun., noon-5 p.m.
Place: 1524 Kanawha Blvd.
Contact: (304) 345-0087

Governor's Mansion

This traditional Georgian Colonial structure is completely redecorated in a most elegant way, from the spacious foyer to the warm, yet formal living room with its antique Japanese screens.
Time: Thurs.-Fri., 9:30-11:30 a.m.
Place: Kanawha Blvd., Capitol Complex.
Contact: (304) 348-3588

Two-Ton Chandelier

The 3,300 pieces of a two-ton chandelier sparkle under a dome that rises 180 feet overhead in the Capitol. Each piece must be cleaned by hand every four years. The dome is the largest of any State Capitol in the country.
Time: Mon.-Sat., 8:30 a.m.-4:30 p.m.; Sun., 1-4:30 p.m.
Place: Kanawha Blvd.
Contact: (304) 348-3809

Clarksburg

Italian Heritage Festival

Organ grinders, free opera, bocce games, fireworks and street dancing—typical activities of the annual Italian Heritage Festival.
Time: Late Aug. or early Sept.
Place: Off W. Main St., between Second and Third Sts.
Contact: (304) 624-6331

Davis

Scenic Falls

Blackwater Falls (65 feet) and the 500-foot gorge in a park of the same name lend drama to 16 miles of hiking trails—used by cross-country skiers in the winter.
Place: .25 mile SW off WV 32 (well-marked).
Contact: (304) 259-5216

Elkins

Fall Migration

The area known as Dolly Sods is of interest to birders during the fall migrations. In a single fall season as many as 12 species of hawks can be sighted in higher elevations. In this rugged terrain you'll also find 25 miles of hiking trails. Primitive camping is allowed.
Contact: Dolly Sods Wilderness, District Ranger, Monongahela National Forest, Petersburg, WV 26847; (304) 636-1800.

Scenic Hikes

Stop in at the Cranberry Mountain visitor center for free brochures, maps and information on the over 800,000 acres of the Monongahela National Forest lying along the backbone of the Allegheny Mountains. Exhibits and free films are shown every 30 minutes. The forest offers 75 miles of hiking trails. One trail (3/4 mile) in the Hills Creek Scenic Area leads down a gorge past three falls, one of which tumbles 65 feet. The Highland Scenic Highway also begins here.
Time: Mem. Day-Labor Day, 9:30 a.m.-5:30 p.m. May, Sept., early Oct., Sat.-Sun., 9:30 a.m.-5:30 p.m.
Place: 8 miles W of Mill Point off WV 39.
Contact: (304) 653-4826

Forest Festival

One of the oldest and largest festivals in the East, the

Mountain State Forest Festival takes place in early October when the trees are turning color. Tobacco spitting, free music, woodchopping—dozens of events draw 100,000 visitors each year.
Time: 1st Thurs.-Sat. in Oct.
Place: Downtown.
Contact: (304) 636-1824

Cranberry Glades

Unusual this far south, the cranberry glades are a botanical oddity best visited in spring. Then the wildflowers are in glorious full bloom.
Time: Best Apr. 15-early June.
Place: Near Cranberry Visitor Center.
Contact: (304) 653-4826

Fayetteville

Spectacular View

Where US 19 crosses the highest single arch bridge (876 feet) in the East, you'll have a sensational view of the New River Gorge, one of the most beautiful in the state.
Place: 1 mi. NW of Fayetteville on US 19.

Grafton

Moms' Tribute

There was a time when there was no such thing as Mother's

WEST VIRGINIA

Grafton

Day. Throughout her life Anna Jarvis tried to spark the idea of a day of tribute to mothers, though she herself was childless. Here Anna's mother prayed and taught. Here also you'll find the International Shrine to Motherhood.
Time: 9:30 a.m.-4 p.m. (closed for lunch).
Place: Andrews Church, on Main St.
Contact: (304) 265-1589

Green Bank

2600-Ton Radio Telescope

Tours of the National Radio Astronomy Observatory begin with a 15-minute movie and end with a free bus tour of the site. The tours include a demonstration of how radio telescopes work. They start on the hour and last one hour.
Time: Mid-June-Labor Day, 9 a.m.-4 p.m; Sept., Oct., Sat.-Sun., 9 a.m.-4 p.m.
Place: Deer Creek Valley.
Contact: (304) 456-2011

Harpers Ferry

John Brown

Tour the area in which John Brown began his famous insurrection for which he was later hanged. Begin with a stop at the visitor center. Here you can see slide shows and get full details on this national historic site.
Time: June-Aug., 8 a.m.-6 p.m.; rest of year, 8 a.m.-5 p.m.
Place: On US 340.
Contact: (304) 535-6371

Horse Shoe Run

Another Contender

Our Lady of the Pines, one of the contenders for "smallest church in the world," draws an overflow crowd at summer services without any effort at all. The pews accommodate 12.
Contact: (304) 735-5236

Huntington

Catch a Star

In the Donald C. Martin Observatory, catch sight of a star through the 14-inch Celestron telescope. On clear nights, this is a moment to remember.
Time: 1 day a month. Call for schedule.
Place: 2033 McCoy Rd.
Contact: (304) 529-2701

Rose Gardens

Only a few blocks from the downtown area, Ritter Park displays its most outstanding feature: two acres of roses. The city adds the newest varieties each year, making this a popular stop-off point. Best from May to early August.
Time: Sunrise-10 p.m.
Place: Near Huntington Galleries.
Contact: (304) 696-5954

Huntington Galleries

A major art museum, Huntington Galleries attracts thousands of visitors yearly. Here you'll find superb exhibits ranging from a firearms collection to Georgian silver and Turkish prayer rugs. The museum is acquiring contemporary glass and is nationally recognized for its Braille trail, part of a 2-1/2-mile nature walk.
Time: Tues.-Sat., 10 a.m.-4 p.m.; Sun., 1-5 p.m.
Place: 2033 Meloy Rd.
Contact: (304) 529-2701

Martinsburg

1789 Home

A severe, sturdy residence of native limestone completed in 1789, the General Adam Stephen House crowns a rocky hill overlooking Tuscarora Creek. The Revolutionary War officer and founder of Martinsburg chose a site that overlooked his sawmill, grist mill and other holdings in the river valley. The three-storey home, surrounded by a limestone wall, has been restored and is furnished in the style of the late 1700s.

Time: May-Oct., 2-5 p.m.
Place: 309 E. John St.
Contact: (304) 267-4796

Milton

Glass Art

Blenko glass has been producing handblown glassware since 1893. From an observation area you can watch molten glass be transformed into pieces of art. There are lovely exhibit areas as well.

Time: Center: Mon.-Sat., 8 a.m.-4:45 p.m.; Sun., noon-4:45 p.m. Glassblowing: Mon.-Fri., 8 a.m.-3:30 p.m. (no work at lunch).
Place: Signs in town direct you to the plant.
Contact: (304) 743-9081

Morgantown

Lead Crystal

Blowing glassware of lead crystal, cutting glassware by hand—two arts you'll see on a tour of Seneca Glass Company, one of the oldest in the state.

Time: Tours: Mon.-Fri., 9 a.m.-4 p.m. Center: Mon.-Fri., 9 a.m.-4 p.m.; Sat., 9 a.m.-noon.

Place: 709 Beechhurst Ave.
Contact: (304) 292-7121

Parkersburg

Bird Prints

The Don Whitlach Wildlife Art Gallery specializes in its namesake's renditions of birds native to the area. Their quality has given Whitlach a growing national reputation.

Time: Mon.-Fri., 9 a.m.-5 p.m.
Place: 1121 Murdoch Ave.
Contact: (304) 422-7622

Petersburg

1,000-Foot Rock

The first warrior able to scale Seneca Rocks is said to have won the hand of a Seneca chief's daughter at this 1,000-foot high mass of rocks, one of the East's most impressive geological formations. Here and throughout the area, climbers find stiff challenges and many pitons are still in place from previous climbs.

Time: Accessible year-round.
Place: 20 miles S on WV 28.
Contact: (304) 567-2827 or 257-4488

Spruce Knob

Spruce Knob, the highest point in the state, is best visited from May to October. (During the winter the forest roads are not plowed.) There's an observation platform for a scenic view and memorable photograph.

Time: May-Oct.
Place: 30 miles S of town off WV 28.
Contact: (304) 567-2827 or 257-4488

Phillippi

Twin-Barreled Bridge

The bridge over the Tygart River near Phillippi is West Virginia's most famous. The white bridge, which accommodates two lanes of traffic, was built in 1852 and is still in use.

WEST VIRGINIA

White Sulphur Springs

Elegant Hotel

Tours of the historic and elegant Greenbrier Hotel will take you in the footsteps of the world-famous, from John F. Kennedy to Princess Grace. This is one of the most beautifully landscaped hotels in the region.

Time: Mon., Wed., Fri., 10:30 a.m.
Contact: (304) 536-1110

Statewide

Free Parks

Write for the free "West Virginia State Parks and Forests" brochure. There is no entrance fee to any of these, making them one of the state's best free attractions.

Contact: West Virginia Department of Natural Resources, Division of Parks and Recreation, State Capitol-SP, Charleston, WV 25305; (304) 348-2764.

INDEX

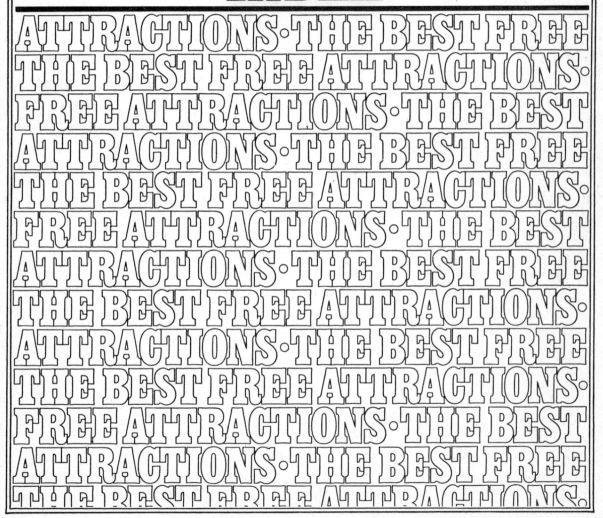

ATTRACTIONS·THE BEST FREE
THE BEST FREE ATTRACTIONS·
FREE ATTRACTIONS·THE BEST
ATTRACTIONS·THE BEST FREE
THE BEST FREE ATTRACTIONS·
FREE ATTRACTIONS·THE BEST
ATTRACTIONS·THE BEST FREE
THE BEST FREE ATTRACTIONS·
ATTRACTIONS·THE BEST FREE
THE BEST FREE ATTRACTIONS·
FREE ATTRACTIONS·THE BEST
ATTRACTIONS·THE BEST FREE
THE BEST FREE ATTRACTIONS·

INDEX

A

African art, see Fine arts, Museums
Aircraft: D.C., 24; Md., 46
American art, see Fine arts, Museums
Animals, see Bees, Birds, Fish, Marine life, Wildlife, Zoos
Antiques: Conn., 5; Del., 13; Md., 43; Mass., 60; N.H., 65, 66; N.J., 72; N.Y., 92, 93; R.I., 111; Va., 127
Aquaria: D.C., 24; Mass., 59, 61; Pa., 107
Arboreta: D.C., 29; Mass., 52; N.Y., 96. See also Plant life
Archaeological ruins and artifacts: Del., 16. See also Fossils, Museums
Architectural attractions: Conn., 4, 6; Del., 12, 14-17; D.C., 20, 21, 26-28; Maine, 32, 34; Md., 43, 46; Mass., 51, 62; N.H., 65; N.J., 71, 72, 74, 76, 77; N.Y., 82, 83, 86, 89, 91; Pa., 107; R.I., 111, 113; Vt., 118, 119; Va., 125, 126, 132-135; W. Va., 140, 144
Archives, national: D.C., 24
Art centers, see Museums
Arts and crafts: Del., 14, 16; Maine, 36; Md., 43; Mass., 57; N.J., 71, 76; N.Y., 91, 96; Va., 126, 127, 137. See also Fine arts, Museums
Auctions: Md., 43; N.J., 72; N.Y., 93; Va., 128
Aviaries: D.C., 26; Mass., 50, 51; Pa., 107; R.I., 110. See also Birds; Refuges, wildlife; Wildlife

B

Backpacking: Maine, 33; Md., 45; Pa., 108. See also Hiking
Ballet: Va., 134
Band music, see Concerts
Banks: N.Y., 88; Va., 133
Battle sites: Md., 45; Mass., 50; Pa., 103, 104; Vt., 117; Va., 128, 133, 134, 137
Beaches: Del., 12, 14-16; Md., 42; Mass., 54, 56; N.J., 70, 72, 77; N.Y., 86, 87; Va., 137. See also Coastlines, Lakes
Beer, see Breweries
Bees: N.J., 76; Vt., 120
Bell towers: Mass., 59; N.Y., 93; Va., 126, 131
Berry picking: Maine, 38
Biking: D.C., 27; Md., 45; Mass., 53, 54, 56; N.Y., 82, 88; Va., 125
Birds: Conn., 4, 6; Del., 14, 26; Maine, 32-34, 37; Md., 42; Mass., 51, 53, 54, 56, 59; N.H., 64; N.Y., 80, 83, 93; Pa., 102, 107; R.I., 110; Va., 127; W. Va., 141, 143. See also Aviaries; Refuges, wildlife; Wildlife; Zoos
Bird sanctuaries, see Aviaries; Birds; Refuges, wildlife
Boardwalks, see Beaches
Boat races, see Contests, Ships
Boats, see Ships
Body surfing: Del., 15; N.Y., 87
Book collections: Del., 12, 16; D.C., 21; Mass., 51; N.Y., 90. See also Libraries, Museums
Breweries: N.H., 67; N.Y., 98; Va., 136
Bridges: Conn., 10; Maine, 35, 37; Mass., 57, 58; N.Y., 85; Pa., 108; Vt., 116, 119, 121; Va., 125; W. Va., 143

C

Camping: Maine, 38; Pa., 108; W. Va., 141
Candy making: Conn., 7; Mass., 54; Pa., 105; Vt., 119
Capitol, US: D.C., 20, 29
Carnivals, see Festivals
Capitols, see State capitols
Casinos: N.J., 70
Cathedrals, see Churches
Caves: D.C., 23
Celebrations, see Festivals
Celebrities: N.J., 70; Pa., 106
Cemeteries: Conn., 6; Mass., 53; Va., 126
Ceramics, see Arts and crafts, Museums
Chapels, see Churches
Cheese making: Vt., 116-118
Children's attractions: Conn., 6, 7, 9, 10; Del., 15, 16; D.C., 24-26, 29, 30; Md., 43, 44; Mass., 57, 58; N.J., 76, 78; N.Y., 81, 84-87, 93; R.I., 113; Vt., 116, 117; Va., 125, 129, 134. See also Museums, Zoos
Christmas tree, national: D.C., 25
Churches: Del., 12, 13, 16; D.C., 26, 27, 29; Mass., 52, 55; N.J., 74, 77; N.Y., 82, 86, 90, 93, 95; R.I., 111, 112; Vt., 118; Va., 124, 125, 129, 130, 132, 133, 135; W. Va., 142
Circuses: Conn., 4, 7
Civil War attractions: Pa., 104; Va., 124, 128, 131-134
Clamming: Mass., 56
Clocks: N.Y., 83
Clowns: Conn., 7
Coastlines: Del., 7; Maine, 32, 35, 38. See also Beaches
Coins, see Money

INDEX

INDEX

Zoos: Conn., 8; Del., 16; D.C., 24-26; Mass., 50, 51, 59; N.J., 72; N.Y., 85, 88, 93, 94; Pa., 107; R.I., 112; Va., 134

Response Page

We are eager to keep *The Best Free Attractions* as accurate and useful to travelers as possible. If you find any changes in times, contacts and so on, or any alterations in the nature of the attractions themselves, please note them on the form below and send them to us.

In addition, if you find any new free attractions that you'd like to see included in future revisions, you can use the form below to let us know about them.

Thanks for your help.

☐ Change in Free Attraction   ☐ New Free Attraction

City: _____   Time: _____

Name of Attraction: _____   Place: _____

Description: _____   Contact: _____

_____   Note: _____

_____

_____   Send to: **Meadowbrook Press**   Dept. FRAT
                  18318 Minnetonka Blvd.
_____   Deephaven, MN 55391

Response Page

☐ Change in Free Attraction   ☐ New Free Attraction

City: _____   Time: _____

Name of Attraction: _____   Place: _____

Description: _____   Contact: _____

_____   Note: _____

_____

_____   Send to: **Meadowbrook Press**   Dept. FRAT
                                        18318 Minnetonka Blvd.
                                        Deephaven, MN 55391

FREE STUFF BOOKS

FREE STUFF FOR KIDS
Over 250 of the best free and up-to-a-dollar
things kids can get by mail:
- coins & stamps
- bumper stickers & decals
- posters & maps

$3.75 ppd.

FREE STUFF FOR COOKS
Over 250 of the best free and up-to-a-dollar
booklets and samples cooks can get by
mail:
- cookbooks & recipe cards
- money-saving shopping guides
- seeds & spices

$3.75 ppd.

FREE STUFF FOR PARENTS
Over 250 of the best free and up-to-a-dollar
booklets and samples parents can get by
mail:
- sample teethers
- booklets on pregnancy & childbirth
- sample newsletters

$3.75 ppd.

FREE STUFF FOR HOME & GARDEN
Over 350 of the best free and up-to-a-dollar
booklets and samples homeowners and
gardeners can get by mail:
- booklets on home improvement & energy
- plans for do-it-yourself projects
- sample seeds

$3.75 ppd.

FREE STUFF FOR TRAVELERS
Over 1000 of the best free and
up-to-a-dollar publications and products
travelers can get by mail:
- guidebooks to cities, states & foreign
  countries
- pamphlets on attractions, festivals &
  parks
- posters, calendars & maps

$3.75 ppd.

Whitman's
THE BEST EUROPEAN TRAVEL TIPS
What the travel guides don't tell about
Europe: indispensible, easy-to-read tips
tell how to avoid tourist traps, rip-offs
and snafus . . . and have the most fun for
the money. **$5.75 ppd.**

THE BEST FREE ATTRACTIONS

THE BEST FREE ATTRACTIONS

THE BEST FREE ATTRACTIONS SOUTH

From North Carolina to Texas, it's a land swarming with surprises – and over 1,500 of them free:

- alligator and turtle stalking
- cow chip tosses & mule races
- free bluegrass, watermelon & barbecues!

THE BEST FREE ATTRACTIONS WEST

Just passing through from California to Montana? It's all free and there for the asking:

- belching volcanoes & miniature forests
- gold panning & quarter horse racing
- vineyard tours and free wine samples!

THE BEST FREE ATTRACTIONS EAST

Over 1,500 irresistible attractions – all free – from West Virginia to Maine (the proper east coast):

- a witchtrial courthouse with evidence
- aviaries where *you* are caged
- the "gentle giants" – and free beer!

THE BEST FREE ATTRACTIONS MIDWEST

From Kentucky to North Dakota, the Midwest is chock-full of free things:

- camel rides and shark feedings
- stagecoaches and magic tricks
- hobo conventions – with free Mulligan stew!

SOUTH

Alabama, Arkansas, Florida, Georgia, Louisiana, Mississippi, North Carolina, Oklahoma, South Carolina, Tennessee, Texas, Virginia

WEST

Alaska, Arizona, California, Colorado, Hawaii, Idaho, Montana, Nevada, New Mexico, Oregon, Utah, Washington, Wyoming

EAST

Connecticut, Delaware, DC, Maine, Maryland, Massachusetts, New Hampshire, New Jersey, New York, Pennsylvania, Rhode Island, Vermont, Virginia, West Virginia

MIDWEST

Illinois, Indiana, Iowa, Kansas, Kentucky, Michigan, Minnesota, Missouri, Nebraska, North Dakota, Ohio, South Dakota, Wisconsin

$4.75 ppd. each

BOOKS BY VICKI LANSKY

Hundreds of parent-tested ideas for the first five years. Includes topics such as baby care, feeding, self esteem and more. **Spiral bound. $5.75 ppd.**

The most popular baby book and tot food cookbook for new parents. Includes over 200 recipes and ideas. **Spiral bound. $5.75 ppd.**

The classic cookbook that helps you get your children to eat less sugary, salty junk food...and like it! **Spiral bound. $5.75 ppd.**